BANISH
YOUR SELF-ESTEEM THIEF

by the same author

Banish Your Body Image Thief
A Cognitive Behavioural Therapy Workbook
on Building Positive Body Image for Young People
ISBN 978 1 84905 463 8
eISBN 978 0 85700 842 8

Starving the Anger Gremlin
A Cognitive Behavioural Therapy Workbook
on Anger Management for Young People
ISBN 978 1 84905 286 3
eISBN 978 0 85700 621 9

Starving the Anxiety Gremlin
A Cognitive Behavioural Therapy Workbook
on Anxiety Management for Young People
ISBN 978 1 84905 341 9
eISBN 978 0 85700 673 8

Starving the Stress Gremlin
A Cognitive Behavioural Therapy Workbook
on Stress Management for Young People
ISBN 978 1 84905 340 2
eISBN 978 0 85700 672 1

of related interest

Helping Children to Build Self-Esteem
A Photocopiable Activities Book
2nd edition
Deborah M. Plummer
Illustrated by Alice Harper
ISBN 978 1 84310 488 9
eISBN 978 1 84642 609 4

Self-Esteem Games for Children
Deborah M. Plummer
Illustrated by Jane Serrurier
ISBN 978 1 84310 424 7
eISBN 978 1 84642 574 5

Helping Children to Cope with Change,
Stress and Anxiety
A Photocopiable Activities Book
Deborah M. Plummer
Illustrated by Alice Harper
ISBN 978 1 84310 960 0
eISBN 978 0 85700 366 9

BANISH

YOUR SELF-ESTEEM THIEF

A COGNITIVE BEHAVIOURAL THERAPY WORKBOOK ON BUILDING POSITIVE SELF-ESTEEM FOR YOUNG PEOPLE

Kate Collins-Donnelly

Jessica Kingsley *Publishers*
London and Philadelphia

First published in 2014
by Jessica Kingsley Publishers
73 Collier Street
London N1 9BE, UK
and
400 Market Street, Suite 400
Philadelphia, PA 19106, USA

www.jkp.com

Library of Congress Cataloging in Publication Data
Collins-Donnelly, Kate.
  Banish your self-esteem thief : a cognitive behavioural therapy workbook on building positive self-esteem for young people / Kate Collins-Donnelly.
      pages cm
  Includes bibliographical references.
  ISBN 978-1-84905-462-1 (alk. paper)
  1. Self-esteem. 2. Cognitive therapy for teenagers--Juvenile literature. 3. Cognitive therapy for children--Juvenile literature. I. Title.
  BF697.5.S46C655 2014
  158.1--dc23
                          2013044132

British Library Cataloguing in Publication Data
A CIP catalogue record for this book is available from the British Library

ISBN 978 1 84905 462 1
eISBN 978 0 85700 841 1

Printed and bound in Great Britain by Bell and Bain Ltd, Glasgow

CONTENTS

ACKNOWLEDGEMENTS

First, I would like to thank the young people, parents, practitioners and colleagues who have inspired me to develop *Banish Your Self-Esteem Thief*. Thank you also to all the young people who have bravely shared their drawings, comments, poems and stories in this workbook. Their aim was to help other young people to realise that they are not on their own in suffering with low self-esteem and to highlight that it really is possible to build your self-esteem and maintain positive levels for the future.

I would also like to thank everyone whom I have worked with at Jessica Kingsley Publishers, especially my editor Caroline, for their invaluable help with my *Starving the Gremlin* series for young people, and for their support of my new *Banish the Thief* series for young people. It is always a pleasure to work with people who are so passionate about what they do. Thank you also to Tina Gothard for her fantastic Self-Esteem Thief and Self-Esteem Vault illustrations used throughout this workbook. It has been great to work with such a brilliant artist.

And last, but by no means least, thank you so much to my family, who have taught me so much about self-esteem throughout my life. To my dad and granddad, who always encouraged me to be the best I could be for me; to my grandma and nanna, who taught me that being happy with yourself for who you truly are is the only thing that matters; to my brothers who are strong, determined and true to themselves; and to my partner, who has always believed in, supported and loved me for who I am – a big, huge thank you!

ABOUT THE AUTHOR

Hi! I'm Kate, and I have worked for several years providing support for children, young people and their parents on the emotional issues that young people like you can face today, including low self-esteem. I have also provided training and guidance for professionals working with young people suffering from emotional issues, and their families. Through this work, it became evident that there was a need for a book aimed directly at children and young people on how to develop positive self-esteem, and as a result, *Banish Your Self-Esteem Thief* was born.

This book will teach you about what self-esteem means, how it develops, the factors that can influence it, the different ways in which low self-esteem can present itself and the impacts that low self-esteem can have. And along the way, you will work through activities that will help you apply this knowledge to your own circumstances.

You will also learn how to build positive self-esteem by filling and protecting your Self-Esteem Vault and banishing your Self-Esteem Thief using a range of self-help strategies. Some of the young people whom I have worked with have courageously and generously contributed their stories, drawings, poems and comments to this workbook in order to help you to see that positive self-esteem really is achievable!

Happy reading and good luck banishing your Self-Esteem Thief!

Kate

Introduction

Do you frequently put yourself down?

Do you frequently doubt yourself and your abilities?

Do you believe you are worthless or not good enough?

Do you see yourself as a failure or useless if you make mistakes?

Do you spend a lot of time thinking negatively about yourself?

Do you avoid going to certain places or doing certain things because of your negative view of yourself?

Do you place unrealistically high expectations on yourself?

Do you frequently focus on your perceived weaknesses?

Do you frequently compare yourself to other people and believe they are better or more important than you?

Do you frequently seek reassurance and compliments from other people in order to feel better about yourself?

Does your negative view of yourself have negative impacts on you and your life?

Do you worry that other people would reject you if they got to know the real you?

If you have answered 'yes' to any of the questions above, then *Banish Your Self-Esteem Thief* is here to help you!

Banish Your Self-Esteem Thief provides self-help tools that can enable you to build positive self-esteem whether your self-esteem is low in general or whether it is only low in specific situations. It can also help you if your self-esteem is currently positive to keep it that way for the future.

This workbook is based on something called cognitive behavioural therapy (CBT) and something called mindfulness. CBT is where a therapist helps people to deal with a wide range of emotional problems, including low self-esteem, by looking at the links between how we THINK (our cognition), how we FEEL (our physical feelings and emotions) and how we ACT (our behaviour).

think   feel   act

Mindfulness originates from the spiritual discipline of Buddhism and from meditation and yoga practices. When we practise mindfulness we make a choice to:

- become AWARE of our thoughts and feelings in the here and now

- ACCEPT our thoughts and feelings as they are without criticising or judging them or ourselves or viewing them as reality

- LET negative thoughts and feelings GO instead of focusing on them over and over and over again.

As you progress through this workbook, you will complete activities that will teach you about CBT and mindfulness in order to help you banish your Self-Esteem Thief and build positive self-esteem.

Because low self-esteem affects different people in different ways and because there are many different strategies that can help people to build positive self-esteem, I couldn't put this workbook together in a few pages! But please don't let the length of it put you off completing it! Working through this book as a whole will provide you with the fullest knowledge and the most opportunities to practise what you have learnt through a variety of activities. However, if you want to make a quick start or feel that certain parts aren't as relevant to you as others, then please feel free to dip in and out of the parts that are most important to you. But don't forget that you can always return to the full book at any time in the future.

For some young people, this workbook may not be the only help they will need. Sometimes, self-help tools alone are not sufficient to help a person to make all the changes and improvements that they need to. In some cases, it is important for a person to seek treatment from a mental health professional, such as a psychologist, psychiatrist, counsellor or therapist. For example, if a person's low self-esteem is particularly chronic; is accompanied by other mental health disorders, such as depression, anxiety or eating disorders; is accompanied by negative coping strategies, such as substance abuse or self-harming; or has resulted from abuse, trauma or victimisation. If this is the case for you, this workbook is suitable to be used alongside such professional treatment. Also, please note that you may need to talk to someone you can trust, such as a parent, relative, friend, teacher or counsellor, if working through this book raises difficult issues for you.

So now you have learnt about this workbook, its purpose, its basis and who it is suitable for, let's get started on banishing your Self-Esteem Thief and building positive self-esteem!

1

What is Self-Esteem?

Step 1 of building positive self-esteem is to understand what self-esteem means. Your self-esteem is...

how you think and feel about yourself.

These thoughts and feelings can involve:

- your awareness of who you are

- how you think about your characteristics and traits

- how you think about your abilities and skills

- how you think about your strengths and weaknesses

- how you think about the mistakes you make

- what expectations you place on yourself

- your awareness of what you want from life

- whether you accept yourself for who you are or not

- whether you approve or disapprove of yourself for who you are

- whether you are proud or ashamed of who you are

- whether you wish you were different or not

- whether you believe you have to change who you are to meet other people's expectations or not

- how you view yourself in comparison to others

- how you think and feel about what other people say about you

- how much you believe in yourself

- how confident you are in your abilities

- how much you believe in your ability to develop and grow as a person

- how worthy you think you are as a person

- how you value your contribution to the world

- how you think and feel about certain situations based on your thoughts and feelings about yourself.

These thoughts and feelings can vary at different times in our lives or across different parts of our lives. For example, Tansy, aged 17 years, thinks and feels negatively about herself in most aspects of her life and has done so for as far back as she can remember. However, Fiona, aged 10 years, has only just started to think and feel negatively about herself in response to a difficult life experience that she has recently gone through, and Craig, aged 13 years, only thinks and feels negatively about himself in certain situations. We call these our 'trigger situations' and they tend to be social- or task-based situations.

Here are some examples of the kinds of THOUGHTS AND FEELINGS that other young people have about themselves. Some of these thoughts and feelings may sound familiar to you.

'All the girls in my year at school are prettier than me. I feel like such a freak beside them.' (Sandi, 15)

'I wish she was my friend. She's so good at everything! I feel stupid compared to her.' (Tess, 15)

'I'm so useless. I can't get anything right!' (Lucy, 13)

'I don't like myself much. I'm such a failure at everything!' (Vinny, 12)

'I'll never be good enough. I'm always letting my parents down. I wish I wasn't me.' (Carrie, 10)

'Other people might be better than me at maths and science, but that's OK as I'm good at music and art!' (Martin, 14)

'Some people in my class tease me because they're good at sports and I'm not, but I don't care. I don't have to be like them. I'm me and that's OK.' (Beccy, 12)

'I might not get As at school, but I'm proud of myself for who I am. I'm a kind person and that's what counts.' (Heather, 13)

'My best friend Max is a much better person than me. He got picked by a Premiership football club to play for their youth team. I just play for the school B team. I'm pathetic; he's a champion!' (Daniel, 16)

'I'll never get a girlfriend. Who would want to go out with someone like me? I'm a nobody.' (Ricardo, 16)

'I start at a new school soon. But I'll never make any friends as I'm such a loser!' (Tony, 11)

'I have a stutter. I know everyone in my class thinks I'm weird because of it. And they're right – I am weird!' (Molly, 10)

These thoughts and feelings can also impact on how people behave and on their lives in general. Here are the same young people describing how they BEHAVE in response to their thoughts and feelings about their bodies. Again, some of these behaviours and impacts may sound familiar to you.

'I started self-harming as a way to cope with how ugly I feel.' (Sandi, 15)

'I would always put off doing my homework because I knew I wasn't as good as my friend at it. So she started helping me with it, but now I let her do it all for me as it feels easier for me that way.' (Tess, 15)

'Whenever I start anything, I just end up quitting before I've finished as I know I'll just mess up at it anyway.' (Lucy, 13)

'I avoid doing so many things as I know I will only fail at them if I was to try.' (Vinny, 12)

'I work so hard to try and please my parents that I'm tired all the time. I get angry with myself when I don't do well enough.' (Carrie, 10)

'I try my best in maths and science at school but I spend all my spare time on the things I love and know I am good at – music and art!' (Martin, 14)

'I just ignore the people who tease me at school and try my best in sports lessons. But I put more energy into the things that I know I am good at.' (Beccy, 12)

'I work hard and do the best I can at school. I can't ask any more of myself than that.' (Heather, 13)

'I'm always asking my mum if she thinks someone will fall in love with me one day.' (Ricardo, 16)

'I don't try very hard at football practice any more as I know I'll never be good enough to get picked for a Premiership team like my friend.' (Daniel, 16)

'I did everything I could to try and fit in at my old school. I would even do things that I didn't want to do in the hope that they would become my friend. I just couldn't say "no".' (Tony, 11)

'One girl in my class says nasty things about my stutter when the teacher isn't around. I just agree with her and tell her she's right.' (Molly, 10)

Some of these young people have positive self-esteem and some of them have low self-esteem. What determines this is how they THINK, FEEL AND ACT.

think   feel   act

You will learn more about the links between our thoughts, feelings and behaviours and how these links help to determine whether we have positive or low self-esteem as you progress through this workbook, as understanding this is key to building positive self-esteem.

But first you need to assess exactly how you think and feel about yourself at this point in time and what impacts these thoughts and feelings are having on your behaviours and on your life in general. This is Step 2 in building positive self-esteem. There is a questionnaire in the next chapter to help you to do this.

2

Your Self-Esteem

When we have low self-esteem, we can sometimes try to hide our 'real' selves from other people. We can also try to hide our low self-esteem from others too, as well as from ourselves, because acknowledging it can seem too painful. But hiding our problems does not help us to overcome them.

So I'm asking you to be brave. I'm asking you to put the mask that you may have been hiding behind down and think honestly about how you view yourself and the impact this has on you by completing the following questionnaire. Before you can address any self-esteem issues you may have, you first have to acknowledge that they are there.

MY SELF-ESTEEM QUESTIONNAIRE

1. **How often do you believe in yourself? Tick which answer applies to you.**

   a) Most of the time ☐   d) Rarely ☐

   b) A lot of the time ☐   e) Never ☐

   c) Occasionally ☐

2. **How often do you feel confident in your abilities? Tick which answer applies to you.**

   a) Most of the time ☐   d) Rarely ☐

   b) A lot of the time ☐   e) Never ☐

   c) Occasionally ☐

3. **How often do you worry about what other people think about you? Tick which answer applies to you.**

a) Most of the time ☐   d) Rarely ☐

b) A lot of the time ☐   e) Never ☐

c) Occasionally ☐

4. **How different is the 'real' you from how you would like to be? Tick which answer applies to you.**

a) Completely different ☐   c) A little different ☐

b) Quite a bit different ☐   d) No different ☐

5. **The table below contains a list of negative thoughts and beliefs that people with low self-esteem can have about themselves. Tick any that you agree with.**

THOUGHT OR BELIEF	I AGREE
I am not a worthy person	
Other people think I am unattractive	
I am a failure	
The first things that people notice about me are my flaws	
I am unattractive	
I am useless	
If I am not perfect, then I am a worthless person	
I am unlikeable and unlovable	
If I'm not perfect, no one will ever love me	
I am not good enough	

THOUGHT OR BELIEF	I AGREE
I must be perfect	
I wish I was someone different	
I would change lots of things about me if I could	
If I was a better person, I would be happier	
No one will ever like me unless I change things about myself	
I am not as worthy as other people	
I am not equal to other people	
Everyone else is better than me	
If I didn't hide the 'real' me, people wouldn't like me	
I need to look perfect for people to like me	
I need to be perfect for people to like me	
I don't have any good qualities	
I don't have many good qualities	
The only way to feel better is to change things about me	
If people knew the 'real' me, they would reject me	
I have too many weaknesses	
My weaknesses make me a failure	
I'm not a good enough person if I make mistakes	

THOUGHT OR BELIEF	I AGREE
If things go wrong, it means I'm not good enough	
If I'm not perfect, my life will be ruined	
I don't have much to be proud of about myself	
I dislike most things about myself	
My opinions don't matter	
My thoughts and feelings don't matter	
I don't matter	
I'm not competent enough	
Other people think I'm worthless	
Other people think I'm useless	
Other people think I'm a failure	
Other people think I'm unlikeable	
Things never go right for me	
Things will always go wrong for me	
Other people's needs, opinions and feelings are more important than mine	
If I'm not good at something, it means I'm stupid or useless or a failure	
People are only trying to make me feel better when they pay me compliments	

6. **Do you lack confidence in yourself and your abilities in any of the situations listed below? Tick any that apply to you.**

SITUATION	APPLIES TO ME
Parties	
Performing or speaking in front of others	
Voicing your opinion	
Taking exams	
School or college assignments	
Certain subjects at school or college	
Asking someone out on a date	
Going out on a date	
Making friends	
Hanging out with friends	
Dealing with conflict or disagreements	
Speaking to people	
Giving someone feedback on something	
Making a complaint	
Asking for help	
Leisure activities	
Sporting activities	

SITUATION	APPLIES TO ME
Speaking to family members	
Working towards future goals and ambitions	
Doing something new	
Learning something new	
Meeting new people	
Meeting other people's expectations	
Dealing with a problem	
Responding to people who treat you with disrespect	
Making decisions	
When needing to say 'no' to someone	
Standing up for your rights	
Other situations (please specify)	
....	
....	
....	
....	

7. **Do your thoughts about yourself and your abilities cause you to feel any of the following? Highlight or colour in any that apply to you.**

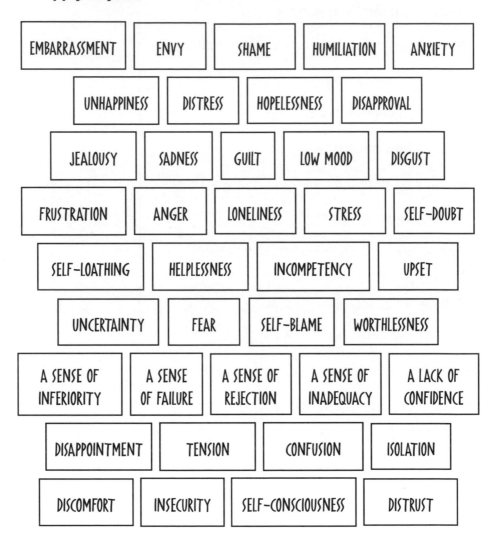

8. **Do you regularly worry about experiencing any of the following? Highlight or colour in any that apply to you.**

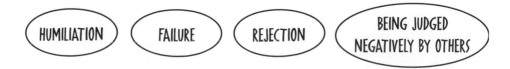

9. **The table below contains a list of what we call 'self-defeating' behaviours. Tick any that you regularly do because of your thoughts and feelings about yourself.**

BEHAVIOUR	APPLIES TO ME
Avoid people	
Avoid certain types of situations	
Put off or avoid doing things	
Put off or avoid making decisions	
Avoid voicing your opinion	
Avoid expressing your feelings, wishes or needs	
Escape from situations that you are in	
Quit part way through doing things	
Hide aspects of yourself from others	
Try to please other people	
Try to be in 100 per cent control of a situation	
Work to excess	
Act aggressively towards others	
Act aggressively towards yourself	
Agree with others even though you don't really agree with them	
Agree to do things you don't want to do to please others instead of saying 'no'	
Say 'sorry' even though you have done nothing wrong	

BEHAVIOUR	APPLIES TO ME
Put yourself down when you speak	
Put your opinions down when you speak	
Avoid dealing with conflict	
Avoid dealing with problems	
Avoid dealing with situations where someone treats you or your rights with disrespect	
Allow others to get away with doing things you asked them not to do	
Use unconfident body language	
Use aggressive body language	
Seek reassurance from others about you and your abilities	
Seek sympathy from others	
Get other people to do things for you	
Do risky or dangerous things to prove yourself to others	

10. Your answers to the previous questions may show that you have negative thoughts and feelings about yourself and that you can act in self-defeating ways as a result. If so, have these had negative effects on any of the following aspects of your life? Highlight or colour in any that apply to you.

SOCIAL AND LEISURE ACTIVITIES	STUDIES AND WORK	FRIENDSHIPS	GOALS FOR THE FUTURE
PHYSICAL HEALTH	FAMILY RELATIONSHIPS	MENTAL HEALTH AND EMOTIONAL WELL-BEING	ROMANTIC RELATIONSHIPS

11. Do you believe that building positive self-esteem is in or out of your control? Tick which answer applies to you.

a) In my control ☐   b) Out of my control ☐

Your self-esteem can be classed as low if your answers to the My Self-Esteem Questionnaire reveal that you:

- have **negative or unrealistic BELIEFS about yourself,** including the kind of person you should be, the ways you should act, the things you shouldn't do, the things you should change about you, the things you should achieve, the things you should want to achieve, and your worth and value as a person

- frequently **THINK in negative or unrealistic ways about who you are as a person,** including your physical appearance, traits, characteristics, abilities, skills, strengths and weaknesses

- frequently **THINK in negative or unrealistic ways about specific situations or a wide variety of situations** because of your thoughts and beliefs about yourself

- frequently **FEEL negatively about yourself,** such as disliking yourself, disapproving of yourself, feeling ashamed of yourself, doubting yourself and lacking confidence in your abilities

- frequently **FEEL negatively about specific situations or a wide variety of situations** as a result of how you think and feel about yourself, such as a fear of being rejected in certain situations

- frequently **ACT in self-defeating ways** as a result of how you think and feel about yourself and situations, such as avoiding or quitting certain situations

- have experienced **NEGATIVE IMPACTS** in your life as a result.

However, please don't worry if this is the case. It's important to realise that you're not on your own in feeling this way, as the stories throughout this workbook will show.

But it's also really important to realise that your self-esteem can change and it can be made more positive. And many young people have managed to achieve this. However, before we move on to Step 3 in building positive self-esteem – namely understanding how low self-esteem can develop – why not have a go at another activity that can help you to understand some more about your self-esteem.

In the next Self-Esteem Box, try showing how you think and feel about yourself, and how you act as a result, through one of the following creative methods:

- Draw a picture.

- Write a song or rap.

- Write a poem.

- Write a short story or play.

- Write a blog.

- Take a photo or series of photos.

- Draw or write down ideas for a short film.

- Draw or write down ideas for a dance piece.

To inspire you, you'll find a poem called 'Everybody Knows' written by Sophie, aged 14 years, a rap by Wes, aged 15 years, and some pictures created by other young people over the next few pages.

SELF-ESTEEM BOX

Let's get creative

EVERYBODY KNOWS

Everybody knows I'm nobody
And nobody seems to care
Nobody bats an eyelid
Whether I'm here or there

Everybody knows I'm nobody
Even when I follow the crowd
Everybody talks over me
Even when I try to be loud

Everybody knows I'm nobody
Does anybody know my name?
Everyone always rejects me
And nobody sees my pain

Everybody knows I'm nobody
And nobody is my name
Everyone else knows
they are somebody
Whilst I'm busy hiding
my shame

I know I need to be somebody
But who am I to be?
I know I can't be just anybody
But how do I find the true me?

By Sophie, aged 14 years

By Nathan, aged 12 years

I'M A LOSER

Try as hard I might
I can never get things right

I'm a loser

Why shouldn't I bail?
As every time I try to
do something I fail

I'm a loser

Other boys are all that
I'm useless and fat

I'm a loser

To girls I can barely speak
So they all see me as a freak

I'm a loser

If only I was someone
other than me
I could be as successful as
my parents want me to be

But I'm me
And a loser I will always be

By Wes, aged 15 years

By Maisy, aged 16 years

IDIOT

HIDEOUS
ASHAMED
TERRIBLE
EMOTIONAL WRECK

WORTHLESS
HOPELESS
OF NO USE

INFERIOR

ABSURD
MISFIT

By Tess, aged 13 years

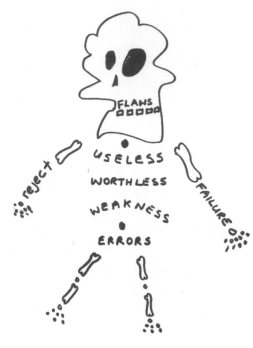

By Mike, aged 11 years

And here's a final method for helping you to become more aware of your self-esteem...

My Self-Esteem Diary.

Completing this diary on occasions will help you to become more aware of how you think and feel about yourself and what behaviours and impacts this leads to.

MY SELF-ESTEEM DIARY

Date................................

The situation

....

What was I thinking about myself?

....
....

How was I feeling about myself?

....
....

How did I behave?

....
....

What were the impacts?

....
....

3

How Low Self-Esteem Develops

Introducing the Self-Esteem Vault and the Self-Esteem Thief!

Think, feel, act!

think   feel   act

As you saw in Chapter 1, our self-esteem is how we think and feel about ourselves and this leads us to act in certain ways. This view of self-esteem is based on something called cognitive behavioural therapy (CBT), which teaches us that it is how we THINK about TRIGGERS (such as situations, experiences, interactions, people, places and things) that leads to how we FEEL and to how we then ACT, as the model here shows.

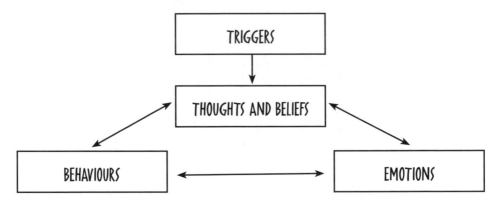

Thus, CBT teaches us that it is how we THINK about ourselves that leads us to FEEL a certain way about ourselves, which in turn leads us to ACT in certain ways. We need to bear this process in mind as we now look in more detail at how our self-esteem develops, including why it can become positive or low. To start us off, let me introduce you to the Self-Esteem Vault.

The Self-Esteem Vault

Let's imagine that we each have a special place in which we store our self-esteem, that is, our thoughts and feelings about ourselves. That special place is your...

Self-Esteem Vault.

Everyone's Self-Esteem Vault has a range of special features.

SPECIAL FEATURE NUMBER 1: IT'S NEVER-ENDING!

It can keep expanding on the inside to take as many thoughts and feelings about ourselves as we like! Unlike your average vault, it will never run out of storage space!

SPECIAL FEATURE NUMBER 2: ITS DEFENCE SYSTEM

Every vault needs a defence system to protect the valuables that are being stored inside it, and the Self-Esteem Vault is no exception. But the difference between a standard vault and the Self-Esteem Vault is that the Self-Esteem Vault's defence system is linked to its owner's behaviour!

SPECIAL FEATURE NUMBER 3: ITS THOUGHTS AND FEELINGS DUMP!

It has a dark, dusty, cobwebby corner right at the very back in which you can dump any thoughts and feelings that you no longer want to keep! You'll learn more about this special feature in Chapter 9.

When we are young!

As very young children, when we think and talk about ourselves it tends to be based on factual things about our PHYSICAL CHARACTERISTICS and our ROLES IN LIFE, such as:

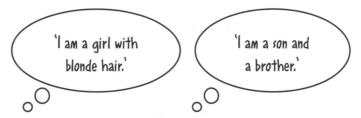

'I am a girl with blonde hair.'

'I am a son and a brother.'

But with each passing day, month and year, we go through more and more experiences in life and spend more and more time with other people. And the older we get, the more varied these experiences get and the greater number of people we interact with. All of these experiences and interactions have the potential to INFLUENCE how we think and feel about ourselves, that is, our self-esteem. But why is this?

Because it is from these experiences and interactions that we start to learn things about our CHARACTERISTICS, TRAITS, ABILITIES, SKILLS, LIKES and DISLIKES, as well as how other people view those same things about us and what kinds of characteristics, traits and abilities are seen as valuable and worthy by certain people in our lives and in society as a whole.

We then respond to these situations and interactions through our THOUGHTS, FEELINGS and BEHAVIOURS. For example, based on these experiences and interactions, we start to form THOUGHTS and BELIEFS about:

- who we are as a person

- whether we like, accept and approve of who we are as a person

- whether we see ourselves as a worthy person.

Depending on the nature of these thoughts, we will either FEEL positively or negatively towards ourselves. It is these kinds of thoughts and feelings that we store in our SELF-ESTEEM VAULT and that determine whether OUR SELF-ESTEEM IS POSITIVE OR LOW.

Positive self-esteem

If our Self-Esteem Vault gets filled with:

- thoughts about ourselves and our worth that are based on facts ('REALISTIC THOUGHTS')

- thoughts that show we are accepting of ourselves just as we are ('ACCEPTING THOUGHTS')

- feelings in response to ourselves that show we approve of who we are ('POSITIVE FEELINGS')

...our self-esteem will be positive.

And the Self-Esteem Vault wants to protect these realistic, accepting and positive thoughts and feelings for us to help our self-esteem remain positive. It does this using its SPECIAL FEATURE NUMBER 2 – ITS DEFENCE SYSTEM. But as I said, how well our Vault's defence system works depends on how we ACT.

In order for it to have the most high-tech and effective defence system available, our Self-Esteem Vault needs us to act in ways that:

- are constructive and positive towards ourselves

- highlight that we accept and believe in ourselves, our worth and our abilities.

These types of behaviours add locks, bolts, chains and security lights to our Vault. And the more locks, bolts, chains and security lights our Vault has, the better protected our thoughts and feelings are...

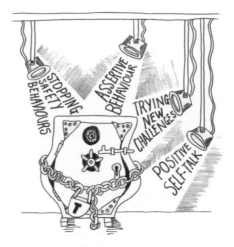

...and our self-esteem can remain positive as a result!

Here's one young person's story as an example.

TANYA'S STORY

Tanya is 16 years old. Both her older brother and sister were straight A students at school and one now works as a lawyer and the other as a scientist. Tanya finds subjects such as maths, English and science difficult at school. However, she is good at music and art. Dancing, playing the piano, singing and drawing are her passions. Her parents praise her skills and abilities in these areas and tell her all the time how proud they are of her. She took her final school exams and did very well in the arts-based subjects, but got much lower marks than her siblings in the other subjects. Tanya feels very different from her siblings, but tells herself that that is OK and that she is just as worthy as they are. She does not dwell on her weaknesses; instead she accepts them for what they are and focuses on what she is good at and what she enjoys. She spends her summer looking forward to studying music and art at college and joins a band as their lead singer.

Low self-esteem

Not everyone thinks and feels positively about themselves all the time. Some people will find that certain life experiences they go through and things that certain people say about them make it more difficult for them to think in realistic and accepting and positive ways about themselves at certain times, that is, these situations have a NEGATIVE INFLUENCE on them. Thus, some people may start to THINK IN OVERLY NEGATIVE AND UNREALISTIC WAYS about themselves, their abilities and their worth at those times. This can then lead to these people FEELING NEGATIVELY towards themselves in certain situations where they question their abilities and worth. And these thoughts and feelings will start to gather in their ever-expanding Self-Esteem Vault alongside any realistic, accepting and positive thoughts and feelings they may have.

For some people, the more they think and feel in overly negative and unrealistic ways about themselves in certain situations, the more they can start to think and feel this way in other situations too. And the overly negative and unrealistic thoughts and feelings start to multiply in their Vault.

As a person's Self-Esteem Vault starts to accumulate more and more of these types of negative thoughts and feelings, they are also more likely to start ACTING IN SELF-DEFEATING WAYS in response to those negative thoughts and feelings. The result is that their Vault's defence system starts to break down gradually over time.

- Chains begin to snap and fall off.

- Old-fashioned locks break and fall off.

- High-tech digital locks get viruses and open.

- The bulbs blow in the security lights and eventually the lights smash to the ground.

Here is an example of one young person whose Self-Esteem Vault's defence system has started to break down.

DERMOT'S STORY

Dermot moves from America to Ireland at the age of 11 with his family. When he starts his new school, he is immediately bullied by some other young people in his class because of his American accent. He practises speaking in an Irish accent at home, but then when he tries it at school in order to fit in and make friends people laugh at him. After a while, Dermot can't get negative thoughts about how his voice sounds out of his head. He gives up on trying to make new friends, believing that his voice makes him unlikeable. He also starts to avoid answering questions in class and pretends to be ill on days when he knows he has to read in front of others in lessons. Dermot believes that his lack of friends is a sign that he is a loser and a failure and that no one will ever think him good enough to be their friend in the future. Dermot's Self-Esteem Vault begins to get clogged up with negative and unrealistic thoughts and feelings and its defence system begins to fall apart. Dermot's self-esteem becomes low.

If your Self-Esteem Vault's defence system breaks down, like Dermot's, it means that your Vault is vulnerable. And the character it is vulnerable to is...

the Self-Esteem Thief!

The Self-Esteem Thief

The Self-Esteem Thief isn't the nicest character you'll ever meet. He thinks only about himself and doesn't have any morals! In fact, he spends his time stealing other people's positive self-esteem! He wants you to:

- be negatively influenced by experiences and interactions in life

- fill your Self-Esteem Vault with negative thoughts and feelings

- act in self-defeating ways so your Vault's defence system breaks down.

And when that happens, he will be waiting and ready to creep into your Vault and STEAL ANY POSITIVE, ACCEPTING AND REALISTIC THOUGHTS YOU HAVE IN THERE...

...and LEAVE THE NEGATIVE AND UNREALISTIC ONES BEHIND!

The result is...

low self-esteem

and

negative impacts on you and your life.

And the more negative impacts your low self-esteem has on you and your life the more likely it is that you:

- will continue to fill your Self-Esteem Vault with negative thoughts and feelings about yourself and that these will multiply and take over your Vault

- will keep behaving in self-defeating ways, leaving your vault's defence system in tatters!

And the more you behave in these ways:

- the worse you are likely to feel about yourself

- the more unrealistic and overly negative your thoughts will become

- the more likely you are to be negatively influenced by life experiences and interactions with others, as well as by other potential influences that we will look at in the next chapter.

And that's exactly what the Self-Esteem Thief wants. He wants:

- your defence system to remain in tatters

- you to think negative thoughts so that the positive, realistic and accepting ones you used to have in your Vault remain with him instead!

- you to get stuck in A VICIOUS CYCLE OF LOW SELF-ESTEEM!

We will look at each part of the vicious cycle of low self-esteem in more detail in the next few chapters. But before we do, have a go at drawing your own Self-Esteem Vault and Self-Esteem Thief in the Self-Esteem Boxes provided.

SELF-ESTEEM BOX

My Self-Esteem Vault

SELF-ESTEEM BOX

My Self-Esteem Thief

How Low
Self-Esteem
Develops

Influences

As you saw in the previous chapter, how we think about ourselves, our worth and our abilities can be influenced by a number of different factors. Although professionals still don't understand everything about influences on self-esteem, what they do know is:

- how we think about ourselves will be influenced by multiple factors

- the exact mix of factors will vary from person to person, just like the ingredients of one baker's cake may vary from that of another baker's!

EGGS

MILK

SUGAR

FLOUR

EGGS

SOYA MILK

HONEY

GLUTEN-FREE FLOUR

We are going to look at some potential EXTERNAL AND INTERNAL INFLUENCES for the rest of this chapter using stories from other young people, as this is Step 4 in building positive self-esteem. The EXTERNAL INFLUENCES that we will look at are:

- past and current life experiences

- interactions with others

- pressure when performing

- societal messages.

The INTERNAL INFLUENCES that we will look at are:

- emotional or mental health issues

- personality traits

- being different from others.

These all have the potential to be positive influences on us. However, for the purposes of this chapter, I will be focusing on their POTENTIAL TO BE A NEGATIVE INFLUENCE on our self-esteem by...

making us more likely to think and feel in overly negative or

unrealistic ways and to fill our Self-Esteem Vault with such

thoughts and feelings.

But, just because each of the influences has the potential to do this, it doesn't mean that you have to think and feel in negative ways as a result. All these are merely POTENTIAL negative influences. You don't have to respond to them or yourself in negative ways. You have a CHOICE as to how you respond, which you will learn more about as we work through this book. It is making such choices that will banish your Self-Esteem Thief, as you will learn.

Past and current life experiences

My Life so far.

Every situation we go through in life has the potential to influence how we think and therefore feel about ourselves, that is, our self-esteem. But certain types of situations are more likely to influence our self-esteem in a negative way, as they can make us more likely to:

- doubt ourselves and our abilities

- feel less confident

- think that the situations and events imply something negative about us.

These types of situations include DIFFICULT, STRESSFUL, DISTRESSING OR TRAUMATIC EXPERIENCES, such as:

- bullying

- parental separation or divorce

- neglect and abuse

- conflict or violence in your home

- humiliation

- accidents to either yourself or others

- physical illnesses and injury to either yourself or others

- relationship break-ups

- bereavement

- difficult challenges

- any other traumatic, stressful or difficult life experiences.

SITUATIONS THAT DON'T GO AS WELL AS WE WANTED THEM TO OR THAT DISAPPOINT US IN SOME WAY:

- rejection, such as not being picked for a sports team, being turned down when you ask someone on a date or not being invited to someone's party

- not doing as well as you would like at something, such as in an exam or in a music performance

- not achieving something you wanted to achieve

- making mistakes.

SITUATIONS THAT ARE NEW TO US OR THAT INVOLVE SOME KIND OF CHANGE:

- starting a new school or college

- moving home

- a new brother or sister being born

- a step-parent and step-siblings entering the family

- starting a new subject or course at school or college

- starting a new activity or interest

- going through puberty.

Here's how one young person's self-esteem was affected by their life experiences.

JAMES'S STORY

James is 12 years old. His parents separated when he was ten years old. He now lives with his mum four days a week and his dad three days a week. He found the break-up really difficult, especially as he would regularly hear his parents arguing about him. James believes that it is his fault that his parents broke up. He thinks that if he hadn't been born his parents would have been happy. He feels worthless and useless and wonders why they still want him in their lives. James tries to do anything he can to please his parents so that they won't reject him. James's Self-Esteem Vault is vulnerable to his Self-Esteem Thief!

In the next Self-Esteem Box you will find a timeline has been drawn for you. This allows you to write down events that occur in your life in chronological order, that is, the order in which they happen. At the left end of the timeline write a zero and write your current age at the right end. Then along this timeline, write down experiences that you have been through that you believe have had a negative influence on your self-esteem and the age at which they happened. If you need to draw your timeline out on a separate piece of paper to fit in all the events you want to include, please do so.

SELF–ESTEEM BOX

My timeline

Now, in the next Self-Esteem Box, list each of the experiences that you included in your timeline, how you thought and felt about yourself in response to those experiences and any ways that you acted as a result.

SELF-ESTEEM BOX

LIFE EXPERIENCE	MY THOUGHTS ABOUT ME	MY FEELINGS TOWARDS ME	HOW I ACTED AS A RESULT

Interactions with others

Q. Have you ever said or done anything that might have had a negative influence on how someone else felt about themselves? If so, describe this below.

....

....

....

....

....

....

....

....

Your interactions with your family, friends, peers, teachers and other important people in your life can also have an influence on your self-esteem. The way in which your interactions with others can influence you negatively can include:

- learning from the way other people respond to themselves and developing similar ways of responding yourself

- judging yourself, your abilities and your worth based on the comments that other people make about you and about the importance of certain characteristics, traits and abilities. These comments can be made through:
  - teasing and bullying
  - other people talking about you to your face or behind your back
  - unrealistic parental expectations

- talking with your friends and family about yourself in a negative way
- family and peer pressure to change something about you
- criticism from others
- others focusing on your weaknesses or your mistakes instead of praising you for being you
- others unfairly blaming you for something
- others rejecting, embarrassing or humiliating you
- family members comparing you to siblings who are different to you
- parental discipline
- emotional abuse

- judging yourself, your abilities and your worth based on the way that people act towards you, such as:
  - ignoring you
  - being aggressive towards you
  - neglect
  - abuse.

Here's how one young person's self-esteem was affected by their interactions with others.

ANNETTE'S STORY

Annette is 14 years old. She was bullied by a group of girls in her class at school for three years. The bullying started because she wouldn't smoke with them at lunchtime. They stopped speaking to her, said horrible things about her and used Facebook to spread lies about her. Annette feels worthless and helpless. She believes she is weak and pathetic because she didn't feel able to do anything about the bullying. Annette also thinks that there must be something wrong with her otherwise they would never have bullied her. Annette has started to self-harm. Annette's Self-Esteem Vault is vulnerable to her Self-Esteem Thief!

In the Self-Esteem Box below, write down any negative influences you think the following people have had on your self-esteem.

SELF-ESTEEM BOX

Your friends:

....
....
....
....

Your parents:

....
....
....
....

Your siblings or other relatives:

....
....
....
....

Other young people you know:

....
....
....

Your teachers:

....
....
....

Pressure when performing

Taking part in performance activities, such as music, drama and sports, can be an incredibly rewarding and positive thing to do for many young people as it can bring a vast array of benefits in terms of health, well-being, sense of achievement, social interaction, future career options and much more.

However, for some people, taking part in performance activities can bring with it certain pressures that can influence the development of self-esteem issues. These pressures can include:

- focusing on appearance as well as performance within the activity

- unrealistic expectations from coaches, managers, teachers, trainers, etc.

Here's how one young person's self-esteem was affected by pressure when performing.

SHAWN'S STORY

Shawn is 15 years old and outside school he spends his time acting. He has been starring in TV adverts and low-budget TV shows since he was ten years old. He has always enjoyed acting and wanted it to be his future career. However, lately Shawn has begun to question his acting abilities. His agent started booking auditions for bigger parts for Shawn in TV and films. But so far, he hasn't got any of the parts, and he is struggling to cope with the pressure and the rejections. He cannot stop thinking that being turned down means he isn't as good looking as the other males who audition and that he is a bad actor. He begins to believe that he will never be good enough to succeed. Part way through his next audition he quits as he believes the casting directors are thinking how ugly and useless he is. Shawn's Self-Esteem Vault is vulnerable to his Self-Esteem Thief!

In the next Self-Esteem Box, list any performance activities that you take part in currently or have taken part in previously. Then list any negative thoughts or feelings you may have had about yourself, your abilities and your worth in response to those activities and how you may have behaved as a result.

SELF-ESTEEM BOX

PERFORMANCE ACTIVITY	MY THOUGHTS ABOUT ME	MY FEELINGS TOWARDS ME	HOW I ACTED AS A RESULT

Societal messages

Society communicates messages to us about what a 'worthy' or 'perfect' person should be like. These include messages about people's:

- appearance

- characteristics and traits

- skills and abilities

- achievements.

These messages appear to jump out at us everywhere we look and from so many sectors of society, including:

- the media (such as newspapers, magazines, TV programmes, films, music videos, computer games, the internet and social networking sites)

- the advertising industry

- the beauty, fashion, fitness, diet and cosmetic surgery industries

- other retail sectors

- children's products

- the government

- the health sector

- the education sector

- employers.

Thus, we are being bombarded every day with messages about how we 'should' be. As a result, it is hard not to take these messages on board. It is hard not to compare ourselves to ideals of worthiness and perfection or to try to live up to expectations that aren't realistic for us. Here's how one young person's self-esteem was affected by societal messages.

DAPHNE'S STORY

Daphne is 13 years old. Her teachers at school are always talking about the importance of exam results and how young people need good grades if they want to get a good job in the future. Whenever Daphne gets a school report it shows how she is doing in each subject in comparison to other pupils in her year. Daphne struggles at school as she is averaging in a D in most subjects. However, Daphne is great at making things and gets As in textiles and woodwork, but she doesn't believe that these skills are valued in life. She believes that being academically intelligent is the only thing that makes us worthy and that she will never be worthy. Daphne puts herself down all the time. She has also stopped working hard in textiles and woodwork because she now believes that she will just fail at them too, so there is no point trying. Daphne's Self-Esteem Vault is vulnerable to her Self-Esteem Thief!

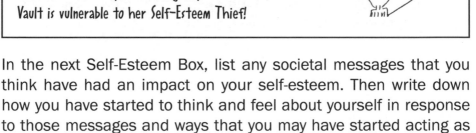

In the next Self-Esteem Box, list any societal messages that you think have had an impact on your self-esteem. Then write down how you have started to think and feel about yourself in response to those messages and ways that you may have started acting as a result.

SELF-ESTEEM BOX

SOCIETAL MESSAGE	MY THOUGHTS ABOUT ME	MY FEELINGS TOWARDS ME	HOW I ACTED AS A RESULT

Emotional or mental health issues

If you have experienced another type of emotional or mental health issue in the past or are suffering from one now, such as anxiety, depression, stress, body image issues or an eating disorder, it may make you more likely to develop low self-esteem. But even if you have suffered or are suffering with some form of emotional or mental health issue, it doesn't have to mean that you will also develop a self-esteem issue. Also, even if you do, it doesn't mean that you can't learn to manage it. Here's how one young person's self-esteem was affected by his other emotional issues.

MAX'S STORY

Max is ten years old and he suffers from anxiety. He worries about bad things happening to him or other people, about going to parties, about doing his school homework, about talking in front of other people in lessons and about being away from his mum and dad when he is at school. His worries have stopped Max from doing lots of things that he wants to be able to do. As a result, Max has started to feel useless and pathetic. He doubts his abilities to do so many things in life now and believes he isn't good at anything. He has also started to believe that his friends are only friends with him because they feel sorry for him. He has stopped going out to play with them after school. Max's Self-Esteem Vault is vulnerable to his Self-Esteem Thief!

Personality traits

Certain personality traits, such as perfectionism, shyness or obsessiveness, can sometimes make us more likely to develop self-esteem issues. However, it is important to remember that even though you may have a personality trait that makes you more susceptible to developing low self-esteem, it doesn't mean that you will develop it. Here's how one young person's self-esteem was affected by one of her personality traits.

JESSICA'S STORY

Jessica is 13 years old. She has always been shy, ever since she was a very young child. Because of her shyness, Jessica doesn't like speaking to other people. She finds science difficult but her shyness stops her from letting her teacher know this or asking questions in class when she doesn't understand something. Jessica is getting further and further behind the other people in her class and her science grades are falling. Jessica feels she is unintelligent for not understanding science and that she is a coward for not being able to tell her teacher that she is struggling. She tells herself that everyone else is better than her and she is worthless in comparison. Jessica's Self-Esteem Vault is vulnerable to her Self-Esteem Thief!

Being different from others

Aspects of ourselves that are different from other people around us also have the potential to have an influence on our self-esteem. These aspects can include:

- physical appearance

- ethnicity

- nationality

- religion

- sexual orientation

- physical conditions, injuries, disfigurements and illnesses

- disabilities

- skills, talents and abilities

- likes and dislikes

- employment

- income.

Here's how one young person's self-esteem was affected by being different from others.

ROBERT'S STORY

Robert is 15 years old. He has dyslexia, which makes him feel different from other people. Robert hates the fact he is dyslexic and works harder than anyone else in his class to try and make up for it and is always feeling exhausted as a result. Despite getting good grades and being in top sets for all his subjects, Robert believes his dyslexia makes him less intelligent than other people. He also thinks that people think he's an idiot when he talks to them because he occasionally mixes his words up, even though they never notice. He believes that he will never be as good as other people and that he will never get a good job or be happy and successful because of his dyslexia. Robert gets very defensive and snaps at people when they mention his dyslexia. Robert's Self-Esteem Vault is vulnerable to his Self-Esteem Thief!

In the next Self-Esteem Box, list any internal factors that you believe have had a negative influence on your self-esteem.

SELF-ESTEEM BOX

Negative internal influences
on my self-esteem

Throughout this chapter, you have learnt about a variety of different factors that have the potential to influence how we think and feel about ourselves, and you have identified which of these factors have had an impact on you. But remember that although these factors have had a negative influence on you and your self-esteem in the past, they don't have to continue to do so in the future. They DO NOT CAUSE you to develop low self-esteem. They just make you MORE SUSCEPTIBLE to:

- thinking and feeling in a negative way about yourself

- acting in self-defeating ways

- leaving your Self-Esteem Vault vulnerable to your Self-Esteem Thief.

But you have a choice to think and feel differently, as you will learn later in this workbook, in order to banish your Self-Esteem Thief for good!

5

How Low
Self-Esteem
Develops

Thoughts

Understanding more about your self-esteem-related thoughts is Step 5 in building positive self-esteem. So let's take a look at the kinds of thoughts that can end up in our Self-Esteem Vault.

Types of thoughts

Our thoughts are made up of two types:

OUR DEEPER BELIEFS	OUR EVERYDAY THOUGHTS
These are general assumptions or rules that we have about ourselves, other people, the world around us and our future.	These are the thoughts we have every single day in response to the specific situations that we go through.

We can fill our Self-Esteem Vault with both deeper beliefs and everyday thoughts. Let's look at each in more detail.

Deeper beliefs

Our deeper beliefs can be:

realistic and positive

or

unrealistic and overly negative.

The internal and external influences that we looked at in the previous chapter have the potential to influence which kinds of deeper beliefs we develop. And over time, these beliefs become fixed in our minds, as we tend to focus on evidence that we think supports our deeper beliefs and we dismiss or ignore any evidence that goes against them. Thus, our deeper beliefs become strict and inflexible rules that we live by and assumptions that we believe in 100 per cent. We very rarely challenge their accuracy, taking it for granted that they are true.

And as a result, we interpret every situation we go through in life based on these beliefs. Thus, the way we think every day about everything we experience and the way we think about ourselves in response to those experiences are guided by these deeper beliefs.

Let's take a look at this further by imagining you have a compass that guides you through life.

YOUR DEEPER BELIEFS	YOUR EVERYDAY THOUGHTS
These make up the compass itself.	These are the compass points you are heading towards.

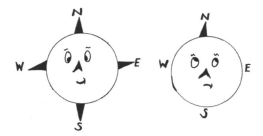

FULLY WORKING COMPASS = POSITIVE AND REALISTIC DEEPER BELIEFS

When you have a compass that is working correctly, it will guide you to the points that you need to get to in order to make the progress you want to make. The same applies to your deeper beliefs. When your deeper beliefs are realistic, they will guide you to think in realistic ways on a day-to-day basis about events, people and yourself, thus helping you to progress through life in a positive way. And your Self-Esteem Vault becomes full of these realistic deeper beliefs and everyday thoughts.

BROKEN DOWN COMPASS = UNREALISTIC AND OVERLY NEGATIVE DEEPER BELIEFS

However, if your compass begins to break down, its needle might start occasionally to stick at a particular direction, such as north, making it more likely that you will go north on occasions, even if you want to go east, west or south. The same also applies to your deeper beliefs. If you start to develop deeper beliefs that are unrealistic or overly negative in some way, you can start to become more likely to think everyday thoughts that are also unrealistic and overly negative, and these start to accumulate in your Self-Esteem Vault.

If your compass's needle eventually gets totally stuck on north over time, you will then always be guided north by it, even if you want to go east, west or south. And once again, the same applies to your deeper beliefs. If the unrealistic and overly negative deeper beliefs get stronger and stronger in your mind over time, until eventually you believe in them 100 per cent and take it for granted that they are true, then it becomes very likely that you will normally be guided towards unrealistic and overly negative thoughts about events, people and yourself on a day-to-day basis.

It is this combination of unrealistic and overly negative deeper beliefs and everyday thoughts that you fill your Self-Esteem Vault with when you are developing low self-esteem. And as you get stuck in a cycle of unrealistic and overly negative ways of thinking and believing, your Vault gets fuller and fuller with these types of thoughts and beliefs, especially as these are the ones that the Self-Esteem Thief leaves behind!

Types of low self-esteem-related deeper beliefs

The unrealistic and overly negative deeper beliefs that people with low self-esteem commonly have in their Self-Esteem Vault include:

- If I'm not 'perfect', I'm a worthless person.

- I need to be 'perfect' in order to be happy.

- If I'm not 'perfect', my life will be ruined.

- I need to be 'perfect' to be liked and accepted.

- If I'm not 'perfect', people won't like me.

- If I'm not 'perfect', I'm not trying hard enough.

- If other people see the real me, they will reject me.

- If people reject me, it means I'm a worthless person.

- If things go wrong, it means I'm not good enough.

- I'm not worthy enough and other people think the same.

- I'm not competent enough and other people think the same.

- I'm a failure and other people think the same.

- I'm unlikeable and unlovable and other people think the same.

- Things always go wrong because I'm not a good enough person.

- If I have flaws, people will notice and dislike me.

As you can see, these deeper beliefs tend to contain the following general assumptions:

- That other people's opinions determine how worthy we are as people.

- That we have to be 'perfect' in order to live a successful and happy life, to be liked and loved by others and to be worthy.

- That the negative things that happen mean negative things about us.

- That hiding or changing our 'real' selves is the only way to make us likeable and to make us feel better.

- That one flaw, imperfection, weakness or mistake makes us unworthy, incompetent, unlikeable or bad people overall.

- That other people think negative things about us because we do.

In the next Self-Esteem Box, have a go at writing down any negative deeper beliefs that you have that relate to your self-esteem in some way. If you struggle to do this at this stage, don't worry, as we will return to this when we look at how we can manage our thoughts in order to build positive self-esteem later in the workbook.

SELF-ESTEEM BOX

My deeper beliefs

Types of negative self-esteem-related everyday thoughts

Psychologists have a name for patterns of everyday thoughts that are unrealistic and overly negative. They call them...

thinking errors.

The following are common types of thinking errors experienced by people with low self-esteem:

- *All or nothing thinking* – Thinking in absolute terms or black and white terms with no shades of grey. It's thinking in extremes. For example, Melissa, aged 11, thinks, 'I'm a total failure.'

- *Over-generalising* – Thinking that what happens in a one-off event is a sign of a long-lasting pattern. For example, Mazher, aged 15, thinks, 'The fact that my girlfriend dumped me means no one will ever love me and I'll always be alone.'

- *Fortune telling* – Making predictions that things will turn out badly in the future and believing those predictions to be true. For example, Tiffany, aged 12, thinks, 'If I audition for the school play, I will make too many mistakes and I definitely won't get picked.'

- *Catastrophising* – Jumping to the worst-case scenario. For example, James, aged 16, thinks, 'I made a mistake in my history presentation in class so I'll definitely get a bad mark and I'll end up failing history altogether. Then I'll never get the job I want in the future.'

- *Mind-reading* – Making negative assumptions about what other people are thinking about you without actually knowing what they are thinking. For example, Jenny, aged 13, thinks, 'I know everyone at school thinks I'm stupid.'

- *Magnification* – Blowing your flaws out of proportion. For example, Gareth, aged 10, thinks, 'Struggling at maths makes me stupid.'

- *Negative comparisons* – Comparing yourself negatively to others. For example, Abby, aged 16, thinks, 'My sister is better at everything than me. I'm useless in comparison.'

- *Unrealistic expectations* – Thinking about yourself in terms of 'I should' or 'I must' or 'I have to'. For example, Martin, aged 15, thinks, 'I should get full marks in my guitar exam' and Fran, aged 12, thinks, 'I must please everyone.'

- *Focusing on the negatives* – Such as in situations, in other people's comments or about yourself. For example, Debbie, aged 16, cannot stop thinking about failing her French exam even though she got As in every other exam subject.

- *Disbelieving the positives* – Treating positive information as false or twisting it into negatives. For example, Kieran, aged 13, thinks, 'My teacher was only trying to make me feel better when he said my essay was good. He didn't really mean it.'

- *Putting yourself down* – Thinking in very critical ways about yourself. For example, Helen, aged 11, thinks, 'I'm an ugly failure.'

- *Self-blame* – Thinking that everything that goes wrong is because of you, even when it is not your fault or responsibility and thinking that everything people say or do is a reaction to you. For example, Tim, aged 10, thinks, 'My dad only left me and my mum because I'm a bad person.'

- *Emotional reasoning* – Thinking that because something feels true to you, it is true. For example, Nicola, aged 10, thinks, 'I feel ugly so I must be ugly.'

- *'I can't' thinking* – Doubting your ability to do something because of how you view yourself and your abilities. For example, Tony, aged 14, thinks, 'I can't try out for the school hockey team as I won't be good enough.'

- *Blaming others* – Blaming other people for how you feel about yourself. For example, Felicity, aged 12, thinks, 'If my mum would let me do the things I want to do, I wouldn't shout at her and feel like a bad person as a result' and Sam, aged 14, thinks, 'If other people said nicer things about me, I would feel better about myself.'

Let's now take a look at your thinking errors. In the next Self-Esteem Box, colour in or highlight which of the following thinking errors tend to apply to your patterns of everyday thoughts about yourself.

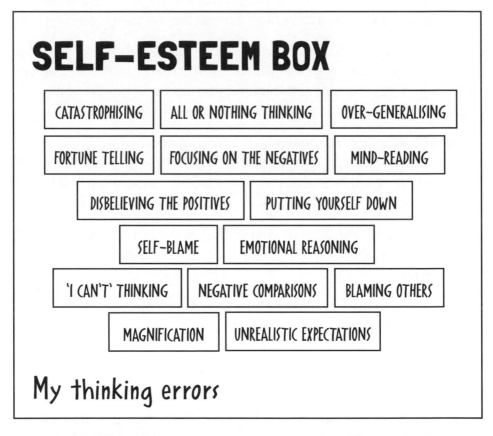

It is normal for all of us to have thinking errors in our everyday thoughts about ourselves every so often. However, when you are stuck in the vicious cycle of low self-esteem, these thinking errors become more and more frequent. After a while, these thinking errors can start to go round and round and round in your mind until it feels as if you can't get them out of there and they clog up your Self-Esteem Vault. And they can then reinforce your overly negative or unrealistic deeper beliefs about yourself and lead you to feel a variety of negative emotions, especially a lack of confidence, self-doubt, and a fear of rejection, failure, humiliation and being judged negatively by others. These also pile up in your Self-Esteem Vault.

We will have a look at more of these feelings in the next chapter. Understanding your self-esteem-related feelings is Step 6 in building positive self-esteem.

6

How Low Self-Esteem Develops

Feelings

If you tend to think in unrealistic and overly negative ways about yourself, then you are likely to experience negative feelings about yourself too. Listed in the boxes here are some of the common negative feelings that people with low self-esteem have in their Self-Esteem Vaults.

	F E E L I N G S	
SELF–DOUBT		FRUSTRATION
DISAPPROVAL		ENVY
DISCOMFORT		HUMILIATION
A LACK OF CONFIDENCE		DISGUST
DISTRESS		SELF–LOATHING
UPSET		HOPELESSNESS
SHAME		UNCERTAINTY
A SENSE OF FAILURE		CONFUSION
ANXIETY		FEELING ISOLATED
INSECURITY		FEELING REJECTED
SELF–CONSCIOUSNESS		DISAPPOINTMENT
LOW MOOD		HELPLESSNESS
SELF–BLAME		JEALOUSY
GUILT		SENSE OF INADEQUACY
FEAR		SENSE OF INFERIORITY
EMBARRASSMENT		PARANOIA
SADNESS		LONELINESS
ANGER		UNHAPPINESS
IRRITABILITY		TENSION
WORTHLESSNESS		DISTRUST
FEELING INCOMPETENT		FEELING TRAPPED
STRESS		FEELING THREATENED

If you think and feel in unrealistic and overly negative ways about yourself, it is very likely that you will then start to behave in self-defeating ways in response to these thoughts and feelings. This then leaves your Self-Esteem Vault vulnerable to your Self-Esteem Thief!

We will look at these types of self-defeating behaviours in the next chapter, as understanding these behaviours is Step 7 in building positive self-esteem.

7

How Low Self-Esteem Develops

Behaviours

A person with unrealistic and overly negative deeper beliefs who is having everyday thinking errors and feeling negatively about themselves is likely to act in ways that fall within at least one of the following behaviour categories:

AVOIDANCE BEHAVIOURS	PERFECTIONIST BEHAVIOURS	HIDING BEHAVIOURS
PASSIVE BEHAVIOURS	ATTENTION-SEEKING BEHAVIOURS	AGGRESSIVE BEHAVIOURS

These are what we call SELF-DEFEATING behaviours as they have negative impacts on us in the long term and leave our Self-Esteem Vault vulnerable to a break-in by the Self-Esteem Thief!

Let's look at each of these types of self-defeating behaviours in more detail.

Avoidance behaviours

A person with low self-esteem can often use one or more types of avoidance behaviours, including:

- avoiding situations, people, making decisions, tasks, etc.

- quitting part way through a task or before they've even tried

- escaping situations that they are in

- putting off doing things – known as procrastination

- not performing to the best of their ability at something.

These behaviours are triggered by the negative and unrealistic deeper beliefs and everyday thinking errors that we looked at in Chapter 5. Thus, reasons for acting in these ways commonly include:

- to reduce the chance of the person experiencing discomfort

- to prevent bad things from happening

- to prevent the person's negative thoughts and feelings about themselves being confirmed by events, situations or other people

- to support their belief that it is better to have not tried or to have deliberately not tried hard enough than to have tried their best and failed.

However, although avoidance behaviours may seem to provide short-term benefits such as those detailed above, in the long term, they do not help and they cause our Self-Esteem Vault's defence system to break down, leaving it vulnerable to the Self-Esteem Thief. Let's look at a story that highlights why.

TONY'S STORY

Tony is 16 years old. All his friends have girlfriends, but Tony doesn't. Tony likes a girl called Sarah at school but avoids making eye contact with her and talking to her. He was partnered up with Sarah for a school geography project by his teacher but he avoided meeting up with her to discuss it because of a fear that she would reject him. Tony doesn't believe he has many good qualities and he doesn't think he is good looking. He therefore believes that no one will ever fall in love with him. However, Sarah does in fact like Tony, but because he avoids her all the time she thinks he doesn't like her. So Sarah starts dating another boy at school instead.

Q. What are the advantages of avoidance for Tony?

....

....

....

Q. What are the disadvantages of avoidance for Tony?

....

....

....

Now list anything that you avoid on a regular basis because of your thoughts and feelings about yourself in the next Self-Esteem Box. And then write down what you think the advantages and disadvantages of each are.

SELF-ESTEEM BOX

SITUATIONS I AM AVOIDING	ADVANTAGES OF AVOIDING	DISADVANTAGES OF AVOIDING

Hiding behaviours

Hiding is another behaviour that some people with low self-esteem use in response to their thoughts and feelings about themselves. This involves hiding their 'real' self from others in some way, such as hiding aspects of their:

- appearance

- beliefs

- likes and dislikes

- characteristics

- weaknesses

- abilities

- religion

- sexual orientation.

It can also involve using laughter or jokes about themselves to hide how bad they really feel. A person with low self-esteem may believe that by hiding their 'real' self, they will:

- please others

- fit in with others

- make themselves more likeable and lovable

- prevent rejection, humiliation, embarrassment, criticism, negative judgement, bullying, etc.

Here is how one young person tried to hide her real self from others and why.

GRACE'S STORY

Grace is 16 years old. Grace is a lesbian, but she hides it from her family and friends because she is afraid they will reject her and judge her negatively. Her family's religious beliefs mean that they think homosexuality is a sin. As a result Grace believes that she is an outcast and a bad person because of her sexuality. She uses words like 'worthless', 'freak' and 'wrong' when she thinks about who she is as a person. Grace is attracted to a girl at school but hides her attraction due to her beliefs and her fears. Grace is determined never to reveal this part of her 'real' self to anyone.

But, although hiding may appear to bring short-term benefits, it also brings long-term disadvantages, including leaving your Self-Esteem Vault vulnerable to the Self-Esteem Thief.

In the next Self-Esteem Box, list any ways that you currently try to hide the 'real' you or have tried to hide the 'real' you in the past. And then write down what you think the advantages and disadvantages of each are.

SELF-ESTEEM BOX

MY HIDING BEHAVIOURS	ADVANTAGES OF MY HIDING BEHAVIOURS	DISADVANTAGES OF MY HIDING BEHAVIOURS

Perfectionist behaviours

Some people with low self-esteem tell themselves that achieving perfection will:

- allow them to feel better about themselves

- make their lives better

- prevent bad things from happening.

Thus, some people with low self-esteem may behave in certain ways in their quest to achieve such perfection, including:

- trying to please other people all the time

- trying to be in 100 per cent control of situations all the time

- working excessively hard at everything they do

- acting in excessively competitive ways

- acting angrily towards self or others if mistakes are made or if things don't go as hoped.

However, these behaviours only lead to negative impacts in the long run and leave our Self-Esteem Vault vulnerable to the Self-Esteem Thief.

Here is an example of one young person who attempted to achieve perfection through their actions.

PAUL'S STORY

Paul is 11 years old. His parents have successful careers and Paul believes he needs to be perfect in order to be as successful as them in the future. His parents have high expectations for him and Paul works every hour he can at his school work in order to please them. Paul is also very competitive and takes part in a number of sports teams both inside and outside school in order to prove himself to his parents. He rarely has any time to relax due to the amount he is doing. If he makes a mistake, Paul gets angry with himself, often shouting at himself and putting himself down. Despite how hard Paul works he never feels good enough.

Q. In what ways did Paul act in order to achieve perfection?

....

....

....

Q. What were the advantages of this for Paul?

....

....

....

Q. What were the disadvantages of this for Paul?

....

....

....

If you believe you need to be perfect, list the different ways that you act to try and achieve this in the next Self-Esteem Box, and what you think the advantages and disadvantages of behaving in such ways are.

SELF-ESTEEM BOX

MY PERFECTIONIST BEHAVIOURS	ADVANTAGES OF MY PERFECTIONIST BEHAVIOURS	DISADVANTAGES OF MY PERFECTIONIST BEHAVIOURS

Passive behaviours

As human beings, we all have certain rights.

Q. List three rights you think you have as a human.

....

....

....

You may have written three of the following or you may have picked other rights which are just as valid:

- to be treated with respect

- to say 'no'

- to have choice

- to be listened to

- to not be physically harmed by others

- to express your opinions

- to ask for help.

When you are assertive, you recognise that your rights are equal to those of other people, you respect your own rights and the rights of others, and you stand up for your rights, needs and values. However, people with low self-esteem often behave in ways that we call...

passive.

Passive behaviours are behaviours that indicate you:

- believe that your rights are less important than the rights of others

- doubt yourself and your abilities

- believe that you are unworthy

- believe that your opinions, needs, wishes and feelings do not matter

- worry about upsetting or not pleasing others

- worry about something bad happening.

And as a result, they leave your Self-Esteem Vault vulnerable to the Self-Esteem Thief.

Passive behaviours include:

- avoiding giving your opinion or agreeing with the opinion of others on a regular basis even though you don't agree with them

- avoiding expressing your feelings, wishes or needs

- acting in ways to please others all the time

- being unable to say 'no' to others on a regular basis

- frequently saying 'sorry' even when you have done nothing wrong

- frequently saying things like 'I think...but I might be wrong' or 'I think...but it's only my opinion'

- frequently putting yourself down when you speak

- frequently making jokes about yourself or laughing at yourself

- frequently dismissing your thoughts, opinions, feelings, wishes and needs as unimportant when you speak, such as 'I wanted to do...but it doesn't matter'

- not addressing the situation when another person denies your rights completely or treats them as less important than theirs

- avoiding any form of disagreement or conflict.

Passive behaviour also involves the use of passive body language in our interactions with other people. Our body language includes our:

- tone of voice

- level of eye contact

- posture

- gestures

- facial expressions.

Now you know what being passive means, try to come up with as many examples of passive body language as you can think of in the following Self-Esteem Box.

SELF-ESTEEM BOX

Passive body language

Your list may have included:

- avoiding eye contact

- quiet or soft tone of voice

- head down/looking down

- fidgeting or twitching

- hunched shoulders

- clearing throat frequently

- crossing arms for protection

- wringing hands

- trembling

- lip biting.

Here is an example of one young person who had a tendency to act in passive ways when with other people.

AMELIA'S STORY

Amelia is 14 years old. She has low self-esteem and doubts herself a lot of the time. On the rare occasions that she voices her opinion, she apologises for what she thinks and says that she is probably wrong. Other people often talk over Amelia as she speaks so quietly. She does nothing about this as she fears confrontation and believes that others are more important than her anyway. Amelia's friends ask her to do their homework for them and she always agrees to do it as she doesn't feel confident enough to say 'no'. Amelia believes that other people's needs matter more than hers.

In the next Self-Esteem Box, list any passive behaviours that you regularly use, any passive body language that can accompany such behaviours and the advantages and disadvantages of acting in such passive ways.

SELF-ESTEEM BOX

My passive behaviours include:

....

....

....

Passive body language that I regularly use includes:

....

....

....

Advantages of acting in passive ways include:

....

....

....

Disadvantages of acting in passive ways include:

....

....

....

Aggressive behaviours

Although it is more likely for a person with low self-esteem to act in passive ways towards others, some low self-esteem sufferers will act in aggressive ways instead. This can be because the person:

- is trying to over-compensate for or hide their lack of self-belief and lack of confidence

- blames other people for the negative way they think and feel about themselves

- feels defensive when other people give them constructive criticism or feedback as they cannot cope with the thought that other people view them in a negative way

- is jealous of others.

As a result, the person goes too far in standing up for their rights and violates the rights of the other person. Such aggressive behaviours can include:

- treating another person with disrespect

- putting down the other person

- verbal abuse

- shouting at the other person

- pushing their opinion on someone else

- meeting their needs and wishes at the expense of another person's

- demanding their own way

- dismissing or ridiculing the opinions, thoughts and feelings of others

- dictating what another person can say or do

- threatening another person

- being physically aggressive towards another person

- taking anger and frustration with themselves out on someone else.

Aggressive body language can include:

- raised tone of voice/shouting

- staring/glaring

- fist clenching

- pointing

- scowling

- entering the other person's personal space.

Here is an example of one young person who had a tendency to act in aggressive ways towards her mum as a result of her thoughts and feelings about herself.

JANE'S STORY

Jane is 12 years old. She feels different from other people at school because of the clothes she wears. Her mum makes her clothes for her and won't buy her the latest fashions that the other girls at school wear. Jane believes she is a weirdo in comparison to everyone else. A few people make nasty comments about her clothes behind her back. Jane believes that no one will ever be friends with her while she dresses like this, despite the fact that she has many great personal qualities. All Jane can think about is how awful she believes she looks when wearing the homemade clothes. She blames her mum for how she feels about herself and shouts at her mum and calls her mean names.

A person with low self-esteem can also act in aggressive ways towards themselves due to the anger and frustration that they experience in response to their overly negative or unrealistic thoughts about themselves. Acting in aggressive ways towards yourself or others will leave your Self-Esteem Vault vulnerable to the Self-Esteem Thief. If you ever act in such ways, answer the questions in the next Self-Esteem Box.

SELF-ESTEEM BOX

My aggressive behaviours towards others include:

....

....

....

Aggressive body language that I use towards others includes:

....

....

....

My aggressive behaviours towards myself include:

....

....

....

Advantages of acting in aggressive ways include:

....

....

....

Disadvantages of acting in aggressive ways include:

....

....

....

Attention-seeking behaviours

Some people with low self-esteem can also act in attention-seeking ways. These behaviours can be influenced by the kinds of negative interactions with others that we discussed in Chapter 4. Attention-seeking behaviours can include:

- seeking positive reassurance and compliments from other people about you and your abilities due to a belief that only other people can make you feel better about yourself

- seeking sympathy from others due to a belief that it will make you feel better

- getting other people to do things for you due to your belief that you aren't capable, even though you are

- behaving in ways that are risky or dangerous or too much pressure for you in an effort to prove yourself to others.

Here is an example of one young person who had a tendency to act in attention-seeking ways as a result of low self-esteem.

NIAMH'S STORY

Niamh is 13 years old. She doubts herself a lot, including doubting whether she is a good enough person, whether her friends really like her, whether she is good enough at school and whether her parents think she is doing well enough. Niamh seeks reassurance and compliments from her parents, friends and teachers several times a day, but no amount of reassurance ever makes her feel better as she doesn't believe what they say.

Disadvantages of self-defeating behaviours

All of the self-defeating behaviours that we have looked at in this chapter may make us feel better in the short term. However, in the long term, they don't help because they:

- keep us focused on what we see as our flaws and our weaknesses

- prevent us from seeing that the bad things we worry about happening are unlikely to happen and that even if they did we would cope with them

- bring increased distress, as the behaviours sabotage our own progress or get us into trouble. For example, if we procrastinate we can run out of time to achieve what we need to achieve

- reduce our self-belief

- reduce our confidence in our ability to handle situations in the future

- reduce our self-reliance and independence

- prevent us from finding out how differently we could think and feel about ourselves if we didn't behave in these ways

- prevent us from finding out that the assumptions we make aren't realistic or accurate

- reinforce our unrealistic and overly negative thoughts as well as our negative feelings about ourselves

- hinder us from living life to the full

- hinder us from achieving what we want to

- hinder us from being our 'real' selves

- affect our relationships with others

- cause distress to others

- lead us to experience negative physical consequences. For example, we can feel exhausted if we work to excess to meet our need to be perfect

- prevent us from discovering more constructive and positive ways to cope with our self-esteem issues

- cause our Self-Esteem Vault's defence system to break down, allowing the Self-Esteem Thief to steal from our Vault!

- keep us trapped in the vicious cycle of low self-esteem!

Now let's take a look at the final aspect of this vicious cycle of low self-esteem, namely the impacts that having low self-esteem can have on us and our lives.

Impacts
of Low
Self-Esteem

Understanding the impacts of low self-esteem is Step 8 in building positive self-esteem. Write down in the next Self-Esteem Box how you think your low self-esteem has affected you and your life.

SELF-ESTEEM BOX

Impacts of my low self-esteem on me and my life

You may have talked about the impacts your self-esteem has had on your:

- physical health

- mental health and emotional well-being

- relationships

- social and leisure activities

- studies and work

- goals for the future.

Regarding PHYSICAL HEALTH, you may have talked about:

- being exhausted from working too hard to please others

- the physical symptoms you experience when you worry about bad things happening, such as shallow breathing

- the physical symptoms you experience when you get angry, such as feeling hot.

For example, Jessica, aged 13, experiences a racing heartbeat, shaking and shallow breathing when she worries about what people think of her.

Regarding MENTAL HEALTH AND EMOTIONAL WELL-BEING, you may have listed some of the emotions that we discussed in Chapter 6. You may have also talked about the links between low self-esteem and the development of other emotional and mental health conditions such as:

- anxiety

- stress

- depression

- eating disorders

- anger

- obsessive compulsive disorder (OCD).

You may have also mentioned how low self-esteem can lead some people to:

- use negative coping strategies, such as drinking, drug abuse and self-harming

- feel like their life is not worth living and to have thoughts about harming themselves.

For example, Lewis, aged 15, started self-harming two years ago to cope with how worthless and incapable he felt.

You may have also discussed the links between low self-esteem and a negative body image. For a thorough discussion on body image issues and how to improve your body image, please see my other book in the *Banish Your Thief* series entitled, *Banish Your Body Image Thief: A Cognitive Behavioural Workbook on Building A Positive Body Image for Young People.*

Regarding RELATIONSHIPS, you may have talked about the various stresses, pressures and strains that can occur in our relationships with others as a result of:

- the other person's worry for us

- withdrawing from interacting socially with other people

- our lack of confidence and self-belief

- a belief that we need to meet the high expectations of others

- our belief that we are unlikeable or unlovable

- doubting that other people like or love us

- dismissing compliments that people pay us

- seeking constant reassurance or attention from others

- our belief that only other people can make us feel better about ourselves

- our passive behaviours

- our need to please others all of the time

- our aggressive behaviours

- our difficulties dealing with constructive criticism from others

- taking out our anger and frustration on others around us

- focusing so much on our negative thoughts and feelings about ourselves that we ignore or neglect the needs of others.

These can impact on our relationships with friends, with boyfriends and girlfriends, with family members, with teachers and with other important people in our lives. They can also impact on how we interact with anyone we meet during our day-to-day lives.

For example, Issy, aged 16, was dumped by her boyfriend because he couldn't cope with her constantly doubting how he felt about her.

Regarding SOCIAL AND LEISURE ACTIVITIES, you may have talked about the impacts of avoiding social and leisure situations because of low self-esteem, which can include missing out on opportunities for:

- enjoyment

- achievement

- social interaction.

For example, Chloe, aged 11, misses out on having fun at sleepovers with her friends because she avoids going to them. She is afraid her friends won't like her any more if they find out she sleepwalks.

Regarding STUDIES AND WORK, you may have talked about a person's performance in their studies or at work reducing because of their:

- inability to concentrate properly due to obsessive thoughts about themselves

- lack of belief in their abilities

- avoidance behaviours, including procrastination

- inability to communicate assertively and effectively with others

- indecisiveness.

For example, Holly, aged 12, is always getting into trouble at school for handing in her homework late. She puts off doing it till the last minute because she is afraid she won't be good enough at it and never completes it on time as a result.

Regarding GOALS FOR THE FUTURE, you may have talked about how the impacts in all of the other areas can combine to have major impacts on a person's:

- motivation to achieve their future goals and desires

- belief in their ability to achieve them

- actual ability to achieve them.

For example, Neil, aged 17, has always wanted to go to university. But when he got offered an interview for a place on the course he wanted, he avoided going due to his fear that he would mess it up and they would think he was useless. As a result, he didn't get offered a place on the course.

Although this chapter has shown you the negative impacts that can occur when we get stuck in a vicious cycle of low self-esteem, please don't be disheartened! It's possible to break out of this vicious cycle and banish your Self-Esteem Thief for good! And the next few chapters will show you how!

Banishing Your Self-Esteem Thief

An Introduction

So far, by progressing through this workbook, you have completed the following steps towards breaking out of the vicious cycle of low self-esteem, banishing your Self-Esteem Thief and building positive self-esteem:

- Step 1 – Understanding what self-esteem means

- Step 2 – Understanding more about your own self-esteem

- Step 3 – Understanding how self-esteem develops

- Step 4 – Understanding about what influences your self-esteem

- Step 5 – Understanding your self-esteem-related thoughts

- Step 6 – Understanding your self-esteem-related feelings

- Step 7 – Understanding your self-esteem-related behaviours

- Step 8 – Understanding the negative impacts that low self-esteem can have.

The next steps are:

- Step 9 – Identifying what you want to change about how you think, feel and act in relation to yourself

- Step 10 – Considering what having positive self-esteem will be like once you achieve it

- Step 11 – Showing yourself compassion.

Let's look at each of these steps.

Identifying what you want to change

Based on everything you have learnt so far about your self-esteem, list in the next Self-Esteem Box what things you would like to change about how you think, feel and act in relation to yourself.

SELF-ESTEEM BOX

What I want to change

Considering what positive self-esteem would be like

For some people, the idea of having positive self-esteem is scary. This is because low self-esteem is all they know, whereas positive self-esteem is the unknown. To help combat this fear of the unknown, have a go at the following activity. In the next Self-Esteem Box highlight what you think positive self-esteem would be like using either:

- words and phrases

- a story

- a poem

- a drawing.

SELF-ESTEEM BOX

What would having positive
self-esteem be like?

Here are some descriptions of positive self-esteem that other young people gave:

Being happy with who you are just as you are

Accepting yourself for who you are

Knowing who you are

Feeling proud of who you are

Accepting that it's OK to have weaknesses and they don't make you a failure

Living your life according to your values

Believing in yourself and your abilities

Celebrating your strengths

Treating yourself well and with respect

Thinking realistically and positively about yourself

Recognising your positive qualities

Being confident in your abilities

Recognising that you are just as worthy as anyone else

Tackling life's challenges in a constructive way

Realising that the 'perfect' person does not exist

Realising that it is OK to be the 'real' you

Below is a poem by Phillipa, aged 16, about having positive self-esteem.

ONE DAY

One day I will realise that it's OK to be me
One day I will stop worrying about what
other people think I should be

One day being me will fill me with pride
One day I will stop looking for excuses to hide

One day I will recognise that everyone is worthy
One day I will realise that even includes me

One day I will recognise I have strengths and abilities
One day my thoughts will move towards positivity

One day I will be realistic about the expectations I place on myself
One day I will realise that you can be successful
without good looks and wealth

One day I will stop seeing myself as a failure and ugly
One day I will face situations assertively and not passively

One day I will have confidence and self-belief
One day I will have positive self-esteem and that will be a relief!
By Phillipa, aged 16 years

Some people confuse positive self-esteem with arrogance. But they are not the same. When a person is arrogant they believe in themselves in an unrealistic way (such as believing they are perfect), they see themselves as better and more important than other people and put other people down. Positive self-esteem involves believing in yourself in a realistic way, recognising that you have equal worth to others and not putting others down.

Positive self-esteem will not prevent bad things happening sometimes, but it will help us to cope with them better and believe in our ability to do so. Thus positive self-esteem brings a whole host of benefits, including:

- coping better with situations
- recognising your capabilities
- believing in yourself
- building your confidence
- going for what you want
- feeling able to try new challenges
- feeling able to face your fears
- being realistic about yourself and your goals
- being assertive
- feeling able to solve problems
- feeling able to make decisions
- being courageous
- having a positive outlook
- taking responsibility for your actions
- enjoying life more
- not worrying about what others think
- and much more!

Showing yourself compassion

You have always had the power to banish your Self-Esteem Thief and build positive self-esteem, but until you picked up this workbook, you may not have known how. So instead, you have acted in the ways that seemed the best thing to do at the time, including the various self-defeating behaviours that we discussed in Chapter 7.

Even though they haven't actually helped in the long term, you did the best you could at the time and no one can ever judge you or criticise you for that. And you shouldn't judge or criticise yourself for it either.

Q. If one of your friends was struggling to cope with something in their life, which of the following would you do? Tick which answer applies to you.

a) Criticise them   ☐

b) Show them understanding and support   ☐

I'm guessing you chose the understanding and support option and you would be right to do so. And understanding and support are what we mean when we talk about compassion. So why not show yourself this same compassion? It's OK to struggle sometimes – you are not a failure if you do. And you shouldn't beat yourself up about it if you do.

By understanding that it's OK to struggle sometimes, by showing yourself compassion and by letting go of the urges to criticise yourself for the situation you have ended up in, you will free yourself up to focus on the last two steps towards building positive self-esteem, which are:

- Step 12 – Managing your thoughts

- Step 13 – Managing your behaviours.

Q. So why is it that these are the last two steps in building positive self-esteem?
Because building positive self-esteem isn't about changing who you are, it's about changing how you think about who you are and changing your behaviours as a result. Positive self-esteem is based on how you think about yourself, which is then reinforced by how you act. And you have A CHOICE TO CHANGE HOW YOU THINK AND HOW YOU ACT:

- You can make a choice to start THINKING IN REALISTIC AND ACCEPTING AND POSITIVE WAYS about yourself and in response to situations.

- And if you do, you are then more likely to start FEELING MORE POSITIVELY towards yourself.

- As a result, you are filling your SELF-ESTEEM VAULT WITH THESE POSITIVE, ACCEPTING AND REALISTIC THOUGHTS AND FEELINGS.

And do you remember that one of the Vault's SPECIAL FEATURES was A DARK, DUSTY, COBWEBBY CORNER WHERE UNWANTED THOUGHTS AND FEELINGS COULD BE DUMPED? Well, that's where you can push the no-longer wanted, unrealistic and overly negative thoughts too! In the next Self-Esteem Box, have a go at drawing this corner of your Vault!

SELF–ESTEEM BOX

The dark, dusty, cobwebby corner
of my Self-Esteem Vault

You are then also more likely to start BEHAVING IN CONSTRUCTIVE WAYS. This then allows your SELF-ESTEEM VAULT'S DEFENCE SYSTEM TO MEND ITSELF. It repairs its broken locks and chains and replaces the blown bulbs in its security lights. Your Vault will develop an amazingly effective defence system once again, which protects all your realistic and positive thoughts and feelings and stops your Self-Esteem Thief from being able to break in!

The result is...

your Self-Esteem Thief is banished

and

your self-esteem becomes positive!

10

Banishing Your Self-Esteem Thief

Managing Your Thoughts

In this chapter, we will look at how you can manage your thoughts in order to banish your Self-Esteem Thief and build positive self-esteem. This is Step 12 in building positive self-esteem and involves:

- accepting that thoughts are only thoughts

- challenging thinking errors in your everyday thoughts

- challenging your unrealistic and overly negative deeper beliefs.

Accepting that thoughts are only thoughts

Do you remember that I told you a little bit about mindfulness in the Introduction to this workbook? What I said was that when we practise mindfulness we make a choice to:

- become AWARE of our thoughts and feelings in the here and now

- ACCEPT our thoughts and feelings as they are without criticising or judging them or ourselves or viewing them as reality

- LET negative thoughts and feelings GO instead of focusing on them over and over and over again.

So how can all this help with building positive self-esteem and banishing your Self-Esteem Thief?

Well, mindfulness teaches us that we have the power to let go of the thoughts that are bothering us when we are stuck in the vicious cycle of low self-esteem. We can do this by becoming aware of them in the present and accepting them for what they truly are – just thoughts. Thoughts cannot harm us, not unless we let them. It's how we choose to respond to them that matters. We can choose to view our thoughts as reality, that is, as a truth that has to be believed in. Or we can choose to view them as what they really are – thoughts and thoughts only. And let them go!

In the Self-Esteem Box here, write down one overly negative or unrealistic thought that you regularly have about yourself and then write down what you need to accept about it.

SELF-ESTEEM BOX

MY THOUGHT IS...	WHAT I NEED TO ACCEPT ABOUT MY THOUGHT IS...

As an example, here is a table that Paloma, aged ten years, completed based on one of her thoughts about herself.

SELF-ESTEEM BOX

MY THOUGHT IS...	WHAT I NEED TO ACCEPT ABOUT MY THOUGHT IS...
I am stupid	Having a thought that I am stupid doesn't make it true. Thoughts aren't facts. So just because I think I'm stupid, it doesn't mean that I am stupid.

Let's now move on to the next method of managing your thoughts.

Challenging thinking errors in your everyday thoughts

In Chapter 5 you identified the types of self-esteem-related thinking errors that you often have in your everyday thoughts which help to keep you in the vicious cycle of low self-esteem. However, it is possible to challenge these thinking errors, which will help you fill your Self-Esteem Vault with more realistic everyday thoughts, banish your Self-Esteem Thief and build positive self-esteem. Here's how!

In order to challenge your thinking errors you need to use something called...

realistic thinking.

Realistic thinking involves doing what a scientist or a detective would do, namely testing your thoughts out against the evidence. To do this, you can ask yourself questions like:

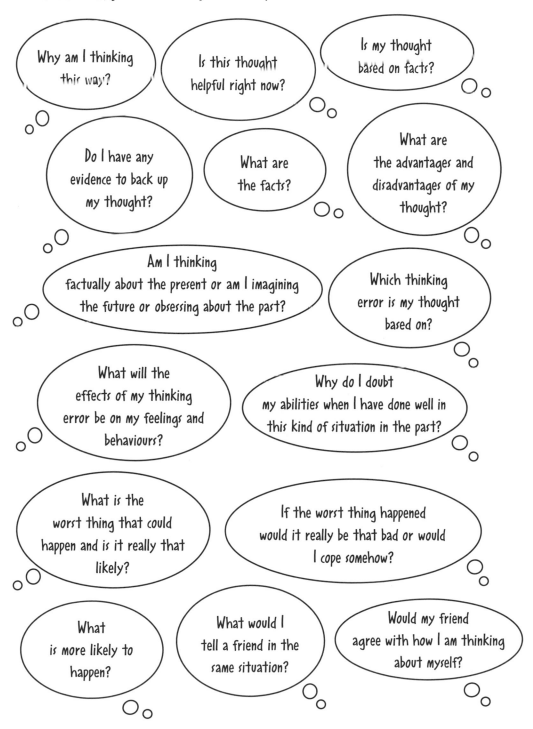

Why am I thinking this way?

Is this thought helpful right now?

Is my thought based on facts?

Do I have any evidence to back up my thought?

What are the facts?

What are the advantages and disadvantages of my thought?

Am I thinking factually about the present or am I imagining the future or obsessing about the past?

Which thinking error is my thought based on?

What will the effects of my thinking error be on my feelings and behaviours?

Why do I doubt my abilities when I have done well in this kind of situation in the past?

What is the worst thing that could happen and is it really that likely?

If the worst thing happened would it really be that bad or would I cope somehow?

What is more likely to happen?

What would I tell a friend in the same situation?

Would my friend agree with how I am thinking about myself?

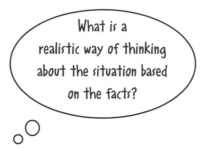

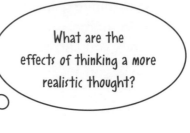

So whenever you find yourself falling into the thinking error trap, try to think about the situation realistically based on the facts. Make sure you aren't being overly negative in some way or blowing things out of proportion. Remember, situations are normally not as bad as we think they are going to be and even if our worst-case scenario actually occurs, we can find a way to cope with it, learn from it and move on from it. Let's look at an example to give you some practice at challenging everyday thinking errors.

JOSHUA'S STORY

Joshua is 15 years old. He is revising for his maths mock exam, but is struggling to understand algebra. He hates it when he can't do something and thinks it makes him incompetent. He cannot stop thinking, 'If I fail, everyone will think I am stupid and laugh at me', despite the fact that all his friends think he is really clever.

Q. Are Joshua's thoughts based on facts? Tick your answer.

a) Yes ☐   b) No ☐

Q. Is Joshua making any thinking errors? If so, which one(s)?

....

....

....

Q. What thoughts could Joshua let go of and send to the dark, cobwebby corner of his Self-Esteem Vault?

....

....

....

Q. What realistic thoughts could Joshua have instead?

....

....

....

If you said that Joshua's thoughts aren't based on facts you are correct. Joshua is making a number of thinking errors, including:

- all or nothing thinking

- mind-reading

- catastrophising

- over-generalising

- putting himself down.

Joshua needs to let go of his negative thoughts and think more realistically about the fact that struggling with one part of maths does not make him stupid.

Some people find it easier to challenge their thoughts by writing them down, especially in the initial stages. This allows you to use these notes again in the future if you have similar thoughts. The alternative thoughts worksheet that follows will help you with this. It will help you to start filling your Self-Esteem Vault with more realistic thoughts, which in turn will help you to develop positive self-esteem and banish your Self-Esteem Thief!

ALTERNATIVE THOUGHTS WORKSHEET

What is the situation?

....
....
....
....

What am I thinking?

....
....
....
....

Do my thoughts contain any of the following thinking errors? Highlight or colour in any that apply.

CATASTROPHISING	ALL OR NOTHING THINKING	OVER-GENERALISING
FORTUNE TELLING	FOCUSING ON THE NEGATIVES	MIND-READING
	DISBELIEVING THE POSITIVES	PUTTING YOURSELF DOWN
	SELF-BLAME	EMOTIONAL REASONING
'I CAN'T' THINKING	NEGATIVE COMPARISONS	BLAMING OTHERS
	MAGNIFICATION	UNREALISTIC EXPECTATIONS

What facts and evidence do I need to be aware of?

....

....

....

....

Are my thoughts based on these facts and evidence? Tick which answer applies to you.

   a) Yes   ☐   b) No   ☐

How can I think more realistically based on these facts and evidence in order to banish my Self-Esteem Thief?

....

....

....

....

Challenging your unrealistic and overly negative deeper beliefs

Once you have become practised at challenging the thinking errors in your everyday thoughts, it is time to start challenging any similar distortions in your deeper beliefs. Challenging unrealistic and overly negative deeper beliefs involves:

- identifying what your deeper beliefs are

- assessing which are unrealistic or overly negative

- developing alternative more realistic beliefs based on evidence.

IDENTIFYING WHAT YOUR DEEPER BELIEFS ARE

You completed an activity in Chapter 5 where you were asked to identify your self-esteem-related deeper beliefs. Re-write your deeper beliefs in the next Self-Esteem Box. As you get practised at noticing your unrealistic or overly negative everyday thoughts in order to challenge them, you may start to notice patterns and themes to them. These patterns and themes will indicate other deeper beliefs you have that you can add to the Self-Esteem Box at any time.

SELF-ESTEEM BOX

My deeper beliefs

Assessing which deeper beliefs are unrealistic or overly negative

In order to assess which of your deeper beliefs are unrealistic or overly negative you need to use the same realistic thinking approach that you took for the thinking errors. So, in a nutshell, you need to assess the evidence. Again you can ask yourself a range of questions to help you test your beliefs, including:

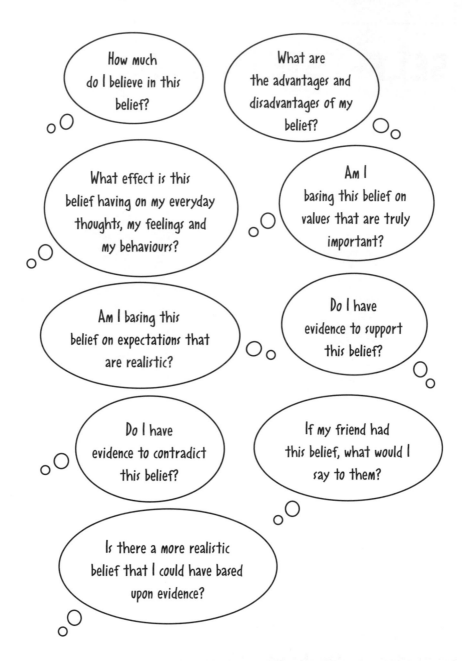

The following Deeper Beliefs Worksheet can help you with assessing your beliefs and with developing new ones to fill your Self-Esteem Vault with. Try completing the questions in this worksheet for each of your deeper beliefs that you believe need challenging.

DEEPER BELIEFS WORKSHEET

My existing deeper belief is:

....

The evidence that supports this belief is:

....

....

The evidence that contradicts this belief is:

....

....

An alternative deeper belief could be:

....

Which is the most realistic? Tick which answer applies to you.

a) Old belief ☐   b) New belief ☐

Which belief helps to banish my Self-Esteem Thief? Tick which answer applies to you.

a) Old belief ☐   b) New belief ☐

Do you remember Joshua, aged 15, who was struggling with algebra? Here is an example of a Deeper Beliefs Worksheet that he completed after his mock exam.

JOSHUA'S DEEPER BELIEFS WORKSHEET

My existing deeper belief is:

If I'm not perfect at all my subjects, I'm stupid.

The evidence that supports this belief is:

My teacher told me I should be getting an A in maths but I got a C in my mock exam.

The evidence that contradicts this belief is:

I got a C in one exam and one exam only.

I have got Bs in maths in the past.

I get good grades in all my other subjects.

No one is perfect and everyone has a school subject that they aren't as good at.

An alternative deeper belief could be:

If I do my best at school I should be proud of me.

Which is the most realistic?

a) New belief

Which belief helps to banish my Self-Esteem Thief?

a) New belief

DEVELOPING ALTERNATIVE DEEPER BELIEFS BASED ON EVIDENCE

As stated earlier in the chapter, your existing deeper beliefs have more than likely been influenced by some of the factors that we looked at in Chapter 4. Thus, in order to help you with your quest to fill your Self-Esteem Vault with more realistic beliefs, it can be helpful to think about the following areas:

- We are all worthy and equal.

- Perfection doesn't exist.

- Mistakes and weaknesses do not equal failure.

- It's OK to be different.

- Who we are is not the problem.

- We don't know what other people are thinking.

- Other people's opinions are not facts.

- We can't please everyone all of the time.

- The past doesn't have to equal the present or the future.

- We need to see the bigger picture of ourselves.

- We must be true to our 'real' selves.

- Knowing your values, aspirations and the things you are grateful for will help you to be the 'real' you.

We are all worthy and equal

Many people with low self-esteem see themselves as unworthy or not as worthy as other people. However, just because someone is better at something than you, it doesn't make them a more worthy person than you or more important than you. It doesn't mean their contribution to this world is more valuable than yours. Everyone who exists on this planet is worthy and equal. You don't need to change who you are to create your self-worth because you are already a person of worth by the very fact that you exist.

Perfection doesn't exist

We all place expectations on ourselves and sometimes we try to live up to the expectations that other people have for us in order to please them, to make them like us or to try to fit in. Expectations can involve believing that you need to:

- achieve a particular thing

- act in a particular way

- be a particular type of person

- look a certain way.

Many people with low self-esteem can place expectations on themselves that are unrealistic, such as 'I need to be perfect'. But we would never achieve this expectation because no one is good at everything. Perfection doesn't exist!

So in order to fill your Self-Esteem Vault with realistic and positive thoughts and feelings and to banish your Self-Esteem Thief, remind yourself that you can only ever do your best and achieve things that are realistic for you based on your strengths, abilities and current circumstances. And remember, perfection doesn't exist!

In the next Self-Esteem Box, list any expectations that you place on yourself that you now realise are unrealistic and then write down more realistic expectations for yourself.

SELF-ESTEEM BOX

MY UNREALISTIC EXPECTATIONS	ALTERNATIVE REALISTIC EXPECTATIONS

Mistakes and weaknesses do not equal failure

We all make mistakes and we all have weaknesses. They are a normal part of being human. We must learn to accept that making them and having them does not make us a failure. It just means we are human like everyone else!

In the next Self-Esteem Box, list your weaknesses and then write a statement that will help you to accept them, especially at times when you are struggling with your confidence. Jason, aged 12, came up with the following acceptance statement:

'No one is perfect. Weaknesses are normal.'

SELF–ESTEEM BOX

My weaknesses are:

....
....
....
....
....
....

My acceptance statement is:

....
....
....
....
....
....

It's OK to be different

Q. What do you think it would be like to live on this planet if everyone had exactly the same looks, characteristics, traits, skills and abilities?

....
....
....

All of us are different and unique in many ways and that is how it is meant to be. We are all supposed to have different talents, skills, abilities, characteristics, traits, looks, etc. If we didn't, how would we be able to fill all the jobs that are needed in society? Because of this, comparing ourselves to others is a waste of time. We aren't all meant to be the same.

In the next Self-Esteem Box produce either a:

- short story

- poem

- song or rap

- blog

- dance piece

- play

- drawing

- poster

- photograph(s)

...that celebrates differences between humans. You can also produce this on your computer or on separate pieces of paper if you prefer.

SELF-ESTEEM BOX

Celebrate our differences

Who we are is not the problem

A common belief held by people with low self-esteem is that who they are as a person is causing all their problems. However, as you have learnt, there is a difference between your self-esteem and who you are. It is how you think, feel and act towards yourself that determines if you have positive or low self-esteem, not who you actually are. No matter what your characteristics, traits, skills, abilities, weaknesses and talents are, you can have either positive or low self-esteem. Here is an example that highlights this further.

GEORGIA'S STORY

Georgia is 13 years old. She is tall, slim and in the swimming team. She plays piano and violin. She gets good grades and has lots of friends. Her parents are extremely proud of her. But Georgia is scared every day about messing up and letting everyone down. She feels as if she will never be as talented as her mum, who is brilliant at everything in Georgia's eyes.

We don't know what other people are thinking

In the next Self-Esteem Box, list any disadvantages you can come up with of worrying about what other people think.

SELF-ESTEEM BOX

Disadvantages of worrying about

what other people think

Unless you have mind-reading super powers, you actually have no idea what other people are thinking about you and your abilities. And yet, we often worry about what other people think, and predict what they are thinking at times – the 'mind-reading' thinking error.

Q. Why do we rarely predict that people are thinking positive things about us?

....

Remember, other people rarely judge you as harshly as you judge yourself. We are normally our own worst critics, as the following activity will show. In the next Self-Esteem Box, write down how you think other people see you.

SELF-ESTEEM BOX

How I think other people see me

Then ask two people whom you trust to describe how they see you.

Q. What do the differences between how they see you and how you think people see you show you?

....

....

....

....

Other people's opinions are not facts

It's important to remember that even if someone does think or say something negative about you, it doesn't make it fact! And just because one person may reject you in some way, it doesn't make you unlikeable or unlovable, or a bad or worthless person. That person has formed their own personal opinion about you, but that does not mean that they have objectively assessed your character based on fact. It is just their opinion. And just because someone may give you constructive criticism, it is not the end of the world.

We can't please everyone all of the time

You can't please all of the people all of the time because you're not responsible for how other people feel. You can only control how you feel. Not pleasing others doesn't make you a bad person. And focusing more on what you want from your life doesn't either! In fact, doing the latter will help you to:

- learn more about the 'real' you

- put more realistic and positive thoughts and feelings in your Self-Esteem Vault

- build positive self-esteem

- banish your Self-Esteem Thief!

In the next Self-Esteem Box, list at least five things that you want to achieve in the next year because you want to and not because you think other people would approve of them.

SELF-ESTEEM BOX

Things I want to achieve in the future

The past doesn't have to equal the present or the future

Past events are merely indicators of what happened at that point in our lives, not predictors of the future. It is important to think factually about the present instead of worrying about the past or trying to predict the future! And remember that you can't predict your whole future based on one specific event!

We need to see the bigger picture of ourselves

You cannot define yourself solely on one perceived weakness or flaw. Yes, your weaknesses and flaws make up part of who you are, but so do all your positive characteristics, traits, talents, skills and abilities. And yes, we all have them and you are no exception! You will have achieved many different things in your life that you can be proud of too!

Thus it's important always to focus on the bigger picture about yourself instead of just on one or two specific aspects. It's not about looking at yourself through rose-tinted glasses for the sake of it. It's about looking at yourself positively based on what is factual and therefore realistic. By recognising all these other aspects of yourself, you will learn to place less importance on your weaknesses as determining factors in your self-worth and by doing so you will be able to:

- fill your Self-Esteem Vault with more realistic and positive thoughts and feelings

- build your self-esteem

- banish your Self-Esteem Thief!

Here are some activities to help you to do this. Some people with low self-esteem struggle to complete some of these activities at first, but it is important to keep working on them.

In the next Self-Esteem Box, list ten positive things about yourself and write down a piece of evidence to back up each statement. To give you an example, here are two things that Felix, aged 15 years, said about himself with accompanying evidence.

'I am a kind person because I help my friends through their problems.'

'I am a good swimmer because I won three competitions last year.'

SELF-ESTEEM BOX

POSITIVES ABOUT ME	SUPPORTING EVIDENCE

Now list at least three things you have achieved in your life so far and write down at least one positive thing that each achievement shows you about you in the next Self-Esteem Box.

SELF-ESTEEM BOX

MY ACHIEVEMENTS	POSITIVE THINGS THEY SHOW ME ABOUT ME

It can be helpful to keep a daily achievements diary in which you can record things you have achieved that day and what they show you about yourself.

In the next Self-Esteem Box, write down at least five strengths that you think you have that can help you to face situations in life.

SELF-ESTEEM BOX

My strengths

Now write down at least three things you believe you are good at in the next Self-Esteem Box.

SELF-ESTEEM BOX

Things I'm good at

Now write down your likes and dislikes in the Self-Esteem Box below.

SELF-ESTEEM BOX

MY LIKES	MY DISLIKES

Next, in the Self-Esteem Box below, write down at least five things that make you a likeable person.

SELF-ESTEEM BOX

Things that make me a likeable person

Now write down at least three things you like about how you look in the next Self-Esteem Box.

SELF-ESTEEM BOX

Things I like about how I look

In the next Self-Esteem Box, write down some compliments that people have paid you. Although your self-esteem needs to come from your own realistic thoughts and feelings about you and not the opinions of others, it can help sometimes to remind yourself of the good things that people see in you when you are struggling to see them yourself.

SELF-ESTEEM BOX

Compliments people have paid me

Now answer the questions about your life roles in the next Self-Esteem Box.

SELF-ESTEEM BOX

What kind of...
Friend am I?

....
....
....

Son/daughter am I?

....
....
....

Brother/sister am I?

....
....
....

Boyfriend/girlfriend am I?

....
....
....

Student am I?

....
....
....

Remember to focus on the positives about yourself in these roles and remember that it's OK to have weaknesses too.

Finally, based on everything you've come up with so far, write down five positive statements about yourself in the next Self-Esteem Box. Remember, we call these POSITIVE AFFIRMATIONS. To help you with this, here are Felix's positive affirmations:

'I am a worthy person.'

'I am a good person.'

'I am a good friend.'

'I am a good listener.'

'I am a kind person.'

SELF-ESTEEM BOX

My positive affirmations

Remind yourself of these regularly. Say them out loud. Put them somewhere you will see them every day. You can even send yourself a daily email or text with them written out!

Q. Do you think how you feel about yourself has changed in any way by focusing more on the bigger picture of you instead of just on your perceived weaknesses? If so, how?

....

....

....

....

Thinking about all the positive and realistic things about yourself in this way will help you to contradict your unrealistic and overly negative deeper beliefs and to develop more positive and realistic ones to fill your Self-Esteem Vault with. This will in turn help you to feel more positive about yourself and banish your Self-Esteem Thief!

We must be true to our 'real' selves

All the activities in the previous sections will have helped you to learn more about the 'real' you. This is the person you are without believing you need to change because of negative outside influences. It is important to be true to your 'real' self and not to the kind of person others think you should be. It's also important not to try to change the 'real' you to fit in with others. You don't need to try to become someone else in order to feel better about yourself. You just need to:

- recognise the 'real' you

- accept the 'real' you

- work on becoming the best version of the 'real' you that you can and that is realistic for you.

In the next Self-Esteem Box, describe the version of you that you present to other people because you think you should or because of a desire to fit in and then describe the 'real' you.

SELF-ESTEEM BOX

The version of me that I present to others is:

....

....

....

....

The 'real' me is:

....

....

....

....

Which version will make me happier and why?

....

....

....

....

In the next Self-Esteem Box, write down activities that you don't already do but would like to do in order to feel more like the 'real' you.

SELF-ESTEEM BOX

Things I would like to do

Knowing your values, aspirations and things you are grateful for will help you to be true to the 'real' you

Many people today view their appearance or their wealth as more important than their health or their future goals or achievements. But this is leading to all the negative impacts that we have seen in earlier chapters. To overcome this, we need to develop alternative values. Our values are things that we view as important in the way we live our lives. They are the things that we measure the success and happiness of our lives by. Learning about our values can help us to respond in ways that reflect these values in situations, and as a result, be true to our 'real' selves. Felix has the following values:

'I see being a good friend as important.'

'I see being healthy as important.'

'I see being successful in my future career as important.'

'I see passing my exams as important.'

'I see being emotionally calm and happy as important.'

In the next Self-Esteem Box, list any values that are important to you. Make sure you are including values that are truly important to you, not just the ones you think other people will approve of.

SELF-ESTEEM BOX

My values

Reminding ourselves of the positive things in our lives that we are grateful for can also help us to stay true to our 'real' selves. Write the positive things in your life in the next Self-Esteem Box.

SELF-ESTEEM BOX

Positive things in my life

Now think about your aspirations for the future and what you want to contribute to this world and write your answers in the next Self-Esteem Box. Only include those aspirations that are true to the 'real' you, not things you feel you should do because of others. Remember that life is full of opportunities. You just need to believe in your ability to see these opportunities and then take them!

SELF-ESTEEM BOX

My aspirations for the future and what I want to contribute to this world

It is hoped that the things you have learnt in this chapter will have helped you to develop new deeper beliefs about yourself and to think about yourself in more realistic and positive ways on a daily basis. Here is an activity that will help bring everything you have learnt together and help you to fill your Self-Esteem Vault with as many of these thoughts and beliefs as you can!

MY SOURCES OF EVIDENCE

Create a scrapbook, box or journal that will be your source of evidence and inspiration for more realistic and positive thoughts and beliefs. It can help to look at this on a regular basis, especially at times when you are struggling with how you think and feel about yourself. You can put the answers to the many activities in this workbook in there, along with any of the following and anything else you want to include:

* quotes that inspire you

* photos of yourself that you like

* your positive self-esteem playlist – songs that inspire you

* your positive self-esteem reading list – books that inspire you

* your positive self-esteem film list – films that inspire you

* mementos that remind you of times when you have felt confident.

You have now learnt about all the different strategies that you can use to:

* challenge and dump overly negative and unrealistic thoughts and beliefs

* fill your Vault with more realistic and positive ones.

Write down your own managing thoughts goals in the next Self-Esteem Box.

SELF-ESTEEM BOX

My managing thoughts goals

Good luck with meeting these goals and banishing your Self-Esteem Thief as a result!

11

Banishing Your Self-Esteem Thief

Managing Your Behaviours

The important final step in banishing your Self-Esteem Thief and in building positive self-esteem is to learn how to:

- manage your self-defeating behaviours

- implement constructive behaviours.

Managing self-defeating behaviours

Here we will look at:

- reducing avoidance and hiding behaviours

- reducing perfectionist behaviours

- reducing passive and aggressive behaviours

- reducing attention-seeking behaviours.

By working on reducing these behaviours, you will help your Self-Esteem Vault's defence system to mend and you will be well on your way to banishing your Self-Esteem Thief!

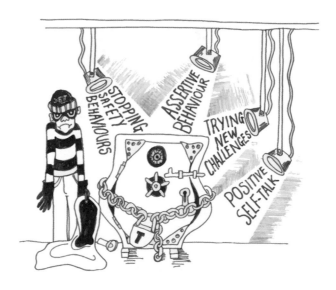

Reducing avoidance and hiding behaviours

When you face situations instead of avoiding them, quitting them, escaping from them or putting them off, you give your confidence and self-esteem the chance to improve and grow. You give yourself the opportunity to see that the negative outcomes that you are predicting are unlikely to come true and that you can achieve the things that you believe you can't. Having a go at something gives you a chance of success, but not having a go only guarantees disappointment and failure.

Think about a time when you did something that you would normally avoid.

Q. What was the situation?

....

Q. What went well and why?

....
....

Q. How did it make you feel?

....

Q. What can you learn from this?

....
....

In order to stop the AVOIDING, QUITTING AND ESCAPING AVOIDANCE BEHAVIOURS, you need to face your fears, worries and distress by gradually putting yourself into the situations that you would normally avoid, quit or escape from due to your lack of self-belief and confidence. Psychologists call this...

graded exposure.

The idea behind graded exposure is that if you stay in the situation that you would normally avoid, quit or escape from for long enough, your worry, fear or distress will gradually reduce until eventually it disappears completely. This allows you to see that there is a difference between how you think and feel about a situation and what actually happens in it. The best way to do this graded exposure is by using an...

exposure ladder.

Here's how to create an exposure ladder:

1. Write down the type of self-esteem-related situation you get worried, fearful or distressed about.

2. Draw a ladder.

3. On the bottom rung of the ladder, place the first thing you want to do to confront your worry, fear or distress. This needs to be the action that you will find the easiest to do.

4. On the top rung, put the final step that you want to achieve.

5. Put other gradual steps on the rungs in between.

6. Start to perform each action on your ladder beginning with the action on the bottom rung.

7. Accept that you will feel some worry, fear or distress at first, as that is normal, but remind yourself that it will pass.

8. Only move on to the next rung when you are ready to.

9. If you feel unable to do one of the actions, try breaking it down into smaller steps and tackle those bit by bit.

10. If you need to repeat a step several times until you feel completely comfortable with it, that is OK.

11. If you are struggling to motivate yourself to complete the steps on your ladder, remind yourself of why you need to, the benefits it will bring and that it will be OK.

12. Use the realistic thinking techniques that you learnt in the previous chapter along with other behavioural strategies that you will learn later in this chapter (e.g. relaxation techniques) to help you along the way.

13. Make a note of what helped you to get through each step in order to complete other steps on this ladder or on a different ladder.

14. Reward and praise yourself for achieving each step.

Here is a story of a young person who avoids a particular situation because of how he thinks and feels about himself. You will then find an exposure ladder for this young person on the next page.

KYLE'S STORY

Kyle is 11 years old. He makes every excuse he can to avoid attending physical education classes at school. He is afraid that everyone will laugh at his birthmark on his leg when he wears the shorts that are part of his school sports kit. He thinks that having a birthmark makes him ugly. He also believes that other people won't want to be his friend if they see he has one. Kyle has now started to feel useless and inadequate because he doesn't have the confidence to attend the classes at school. He is getting into trouble for avoiding them and he thinks that he is a bad person as a result. He hates who he has become.

KYLE'S EXPOSURE LADDER
NORMALLY AVOIDED SITUATION = WEARING SHORTS IN PHYSICAL EDUCATION LESSONS

Get changed with everyone else in the changing room and take part in the lesson.

Get changed into shorts in private at school and take part in the whole lesson.

Get changed into shorts in private at school and take part in half of the PE lesson.

Get changed into shorts in private at school and just watch the PE lesson.

Go to the park with family members while wearing sports shorts.

Wear sports shorts while standing outside own house.

Wear sports shorts at home when with family members.

Look in bedroom mirror while wearing sports shorts.

Wear sports shorts at home in own bedroom.

Pick one of the situations that you normally avoid due to your negative and unrealistic thoughts and feelings about yourself and design your own exposure ladder to address your avoidance in the Self-Esteem Box that follows. Then gradually try to work your way through each step on the ladder, but don't use any other self-defeating behaviours as you complete the exposure, such as reassurance seeking, otherwise you will think you only achieved the steps on your exposure ladder because you sought reassurance during the exercise!

SELF-ESTEEM BOX

My exposure ladder to stop avoiding ....

Once you have successfully achieved all the steps, you can develop exposure ladders for other situations that you commonly avoid. You can also use the same gradual exposure ladder for situations that you normally QUIT OR ESCAPE from part way through or for reducing any HIDING BEHAVIOURS you may use. Completing graded exposure ladders like this will help you to mend your Vault's defence system and banish your Self-Esteem Thief!

Don't worry if a particular exposure situation feels too difficult at first – try preparing for it beforehand. The questions in the next Self-Esteem Box can help you with this. It can also help to visualise yourself achieving a successful outcome in that situation beforehand. You will read more about visualisation later in this chapter.

SELF-ESTEEM BOX

The exposure situation:

....

How I might be thinking:

....

....

How I might feel:

....

....

How I might want to behave:

....

....

How I can challenge any thoughts that might hinder me from completing the exposure:

....

....

How I can cope with any negative feelings during the exposure:

....

....

In order to reduce PROCRASTINATION you need to:

- think realistically and positively about the task and your abilities to complete it using the techniques that you learnt in the previous chapter

- stop making excuses for why you can't start the task

- visualise yourself successfully achieving the task

- start the task or enter the situation that you are putting off

- set yourself a step-by-step plan for completing it and tackle each step one at a time

- reduce the opportunity to get distracted by other things

- remind yourself of the disadvantages of procrastination, such as getting you into trouble for being behind in a task

- remind yourself of the advantages of reducing procrastination, such as allowing yourself to see that you can achieve what you need to achieve

- remind yourself of times when you didn't procrastinate and how well it went

- keep going until the task is complete

- reward yourself for having completed it!

Think about something that you are putting off doing at the moment due to your overly negative or unrealistic thoughts and feelings about yourself. Then answer the questions in the next Self-Esteem Box.

SELF-ESTEEM BOX

I am putting off doing the following:

....

How am I thinking about it and myself:

....

....

Are my thoughts realistic? Circle your answer.

Yes   No

If no, how could I think more realistically to help me stop procrastinating?

....

....

....

How can I change how I behave to help me stop procrastinating?

....

....

....

How can I cope with any negative feelings that I may experience while I tackle my procrastination?

....

....

....

Reducing perfectionist behaviours

The techniques for realistic thinking and developing alternative deeper beliefs that you learnt in the previous chapter will help reduce your perfectionist behaviours. If you recognise that it is impossible to achieve perfection, to meet unrealistic expectations and to please everyone all of the time, then you will reduce the urge to perform perfectionist behaviours in the first place. So:

- Set yourself realistic expectations and goals.

- Accept that if you don't achieve a goal it isn't the end of the world.

- Recognise that you cannot control everything in life.

- Work hard but not to excess.

- Recognise that it is OK to say 'no'.

- Act on your own needs more.

- Do more things that you enjoy, that give you a sense of achievement and that teach you positive things about yourself, including:
    - making time for you every day
    - planning things to look forward to
    - increasing your positive activity levels
    - trying new positive challenges
    - having fun!

All of these will help you to realise that life doesn't have to be all about trying to be perfect! They will also give you the opportunity to feel more positive about yourself and your life, to mend your Vault's defence system and to banish your Self-Esteem Thief!

Q. Name one positive and enjoyable new activity you could add to your life and routine at the moment.

....

Reducing passive and aggressive behaviours

You learnt in Chapter 8 about the rights we all have as human beings and the different types of passive and aggressive behaviours that people with low self-esteem can sometimes display. The key way to overcome passive and aggressive behaviours is to learn about being assertive. Assertiveness is vital to protecting your Vault and banishing your Self-Esteem Thief!

When you are assertive, you recognise that your rights are equal to those of other people and you respect your own rights and the rights of others. Thus, being assertive involves:

SELF-BELIEF	EXPRESSING YOUR OWN THOUGHTS, FEELINGS, OPINIONS AND NEEDS IN A CALM AND RESPECTFUL WAY
RESPECTING THE RIGHTS, FEELINGS, OPINIONS AND NEEDS OF OTHERS	STANDING UP FOR YOUR RIGHTS IN A CALM AND RESPECTFUL WAY

Have a go at answering some of the questions about your assertiveness in the next Self-Esteem Box.

SELF-ESTEEM BOX

List any situations that you feel you are assertive in:

....

....

....

In what types of situations would you like to be more assertive?

....

....

....

How do you think you could achieve this?

....

....

....

To be assertive you need to:

- *think and speak assertively* – thinking and speaking in ways that show you believe in yourself and don't involve putting yourself down. For example, using phrases such as 'I believe' instead of 'I'm probably wrong'

- *act assertively* – such as listening to the other person, acknowledging the other person's point of view in a respectful way (but without having to agree with it), expressing your point of view in a calm, respectful and confident way, and offering potential solutions to problems in a calm, respectful and confident way

- *use assertive body language* – such as good eye contact, relaxed and confident posture, body language that indicates you are listening, such as leaning forward slightly, speaking in a clear, calm and firm tone (not overly loud or overly quiet) and speaking at a steady pace (not too quickly).

These assertiveness skills are helpful to building positive self-esteem in a number of ways, including helping you to:

- show other people that you believe in yourself and value yourself

- have the confidence to make your own choices

- have the confidence to take action in situations

- say 'no' in response to unrealistic pressures or demands

- put your point of view across

- express your needs and wants

- express your feelings

- ask for help

- deal with people who are disrespectful to you

- deal with bullying

- deal with conflict

- reach resolutions and compromises

- respond to constructive criticism in an appropriate manner

- give constructive criticism

- improve your communication skills

- improve your relationships with others

- feel proud of yourself

- believe in yourself

- protect your Self-Esteem Vault

- banish your Self-Esteem Thief!

Think about the last time you acted in either a passive or aggressive way due to your negative or unrealistic thoughts and feelings about yourself, then answer the questions in the next Self-Esteem Box.

SELF-ESTEEM BOX

The situation was:

....

How did I think about the situation and myself?

....

....

How did I feel about the situation and myself?

....

....

How did I behave?

....

....

Were my thoughts assertive? Circle your answer.

　　Yes　　　　　　　　　　　No

If no, how could I have thought more assertively?

....

....

Were my behaviours assertive? Circle your answer.

　　Yes　　　　　　　　　　　No

If no, how could I have behaved more assertively?

....

....

Would thinking and behaving assertively have brought better results? Circle your answer.

　　Yes　　　　　　　　　　　No

Where possible, it can help to think through how you could respond to a situation more assertively in advance. It can also help to visualise yourself being assertive in the situation beforehand. You can also practise assertive body language in front of a mirror, or practise an assertive tone of voice using a voice recorder.

Reducing attention-seeking behaviours

It is important to reduce the attention-seeking behaviours of seeking reassurance, compliments and sympathy, getting other people to do things for you, and doing dangerous or risky things to prove yourself to others. In order to reduce these attention-seeking behaviours you need to:

- think realistically and positively about yourself, your abilities and situations using the techniques that you learnt in the previous chapter

- remember that only you can make you feel better about yourself by thinking more realistically and positively about yourself and your abilities

- remember that you do not need to do risky or dangerous things to prove yourself to other people. You just need to be true to the real you

- gradually reduce the number of times you ask other people to do things for you, while gradually doing more things for yourself

- gradually reduce the amount you seek reassurance, compliments or sympathy from other people by:

  - delaying performing the behaviour for a short period of time, as this will help to reduce the level of the urge to do so

  - setting limits on the number of times you perform the behaviour in one day or only allowing yourself to perform the behaviour at a specific time in the day

- distracting yourself from the urge to perform the behavlour using other activities that you enjoy, that give you a sense of achievement and/or that absorb your attention

- saying 'stop!' or another similar word when you feel the urge to perform the behaviour, which then gives you the opportunity to realistically assess the thoughts that are leading to the urge

- resisting the urge to perform the behaviour completely.

Think about the last time you sought attention from another person in some way due to how you thought and felt about yourself and then answer the questions in the next Self-Esteem Box.

SELF-ESTEEM BOX

The person I sought attention from was:

....

The type of attention I sought was:

....

How could I have managed my attention-seeking behaviour?

....
....
....
....

Now you know how to manage your self-defeating behaviours, let's look at how you implement constructive behaviours.

Implementing constructive behaviours

Implementing constructive behaviours will protect your Self-Esteem Vault, thus banishing your Self-Esteem Thief!

Constructive behaviours include:

- using relaxation and distraction techniques

- problem solving

- talking

- changing your 'self-talk'

- living healthily.

You don't have to try and use them all. Just try those that are relevant to you and your self-esteem. Let's start by looking at relaxation and distraction techniques.

Using relaxation and distraction techniques

You can use simple relaxation techniques, such as deep-breathing exercises, to help you to relax when you're feeling worried or fearful or distressed by situations. These can be helpful when you are trying to face situations that you would normally avoid during the graded exposure or when trying to reduce the procrastination, perfectionist, passive, aggressive and attention-seeking behaviours discussed earlier in this chapter.

Have a go at the following exercises and see what you think. It's OK if these don't feel right to you, as they aren't always suitable for everybody. But give them a go and see what you think. Remember that you can always try other forms of activity/exercise that are aimed at relaxation, such as meditation, yoga and T'ai Chi.

DEEP-BREATHING EXERCISE

Either sit down or lie down on your back. Focus on your breathing. Put one hand on your upper chest and one on your abdomen (just below your ribs). Gently breathe in, and as you do so, notice that your abdomen rises slowly under your hand. Slowly breathe out noticing how your abdomen falls down slowly. Repeat the process, breathing in and out with a slow, steady rhythm. You are breathing correctly if your hand on your abdomen moves up and down slowly but the hand on your chest remains still.

RELAXATION EXERCISES

RELAXATION EXERCISE 1

Close your eyes and imagine yourself somewhere peaceful, happy or enjoyable – somewhere that makes you feel relaxed and happy. Focus on that image, start to build the detail, and for a short time, imagine that you are actually there. Breathe deeply and slowly as you do.

RELAXATION EXERCISE 2

Focus on one muscle in your body at a time, and slowly tighten and then relax that muscle.

RELAXATION EXERCISE 3

Lie on your back. Breathe in deeply and slowly imagining that the breath is coming in through the soles of your feet, travelling up through your body and exiting through your head. Breathe in again and this time imagine that the breath is coming in through your head, travelling down through your body and out through the soles of your feet. Repeat this exercise several times and slowly.

VISUALISATION EXERCISES

- Imagine a calming image.
- Imagine a funny image.
- Imagine you are in a happy place.
- Imagine your worries as visual things being discarded by you.
- Imagine yourself tackling a situation that you would normally avoid, escape or quit from, procrastinate about or behave passively or aggressively in, and visualise what it would look like and feel like to tackle the situation in a calm, assertive and positive manner.

Alternatively, you can use activities that you enjoy to help you relax. These activities may also help to take your mind off the urge to seek attention from others. Have a go at coming up with a list of relaxation and distraction activities that you believe may work for you and write them down in the next Self-Esteem Box.

SELF-ESTEEM BOX

Positive things I can do to
relax or distract myself

Examples that you might have included in your list are:

- breathing and relaxation techniques

- exercise

- yoga or T'ai Chi

- meditation

- hot bath/shower

- listening to music

- watching TV

- spending time with friends or family

- volunteering

- extra-curricular/leisure activities

- going to the cinema

- reading.

Problem solving

Difficult situations and problems can occur in our lives. However, viewing yourself negatively, or mentally beating yourself up in response to these situations, will not make the situation any better. It will, however, lower your self-esteem. Instead, you need to focus your energy on resolving the problem. Problem solving is a way of finding solutions to a problem in order to protect your Self-Esteem Vault and banish your Self-Esteem Thief.

When working out how to tackle a problem you need to:

- work out exactly what the problem is

- think about possible solutions to the problem

- look at the pros and cons of each solution approach

- decide which approach to take and implement it.

Let's see how you can apply this approach to a problem someone else has in the following example.

LAUREN'S STORY

Lauren is ten years old. Lauren's dad was made redundant and cannot find work. As a family they are struggling financially. Lauren had to stay at school when the rest of her class went on a school trip, as her parents couldn't afford to pay for her to go. Lauren told her best friend the reason why she couldn't go and asked her to keep it a secret. However, her best friend told some other children at school and in no time the whole class knew. Now Lauren is getting teased by other children. She feels like an outcast and believes that her friend must never have liked her otherwise she would never have told anyone her secret.

Q. What problems is Lauren facing?

....
....

Q. What solutions could Lauren take to resolve her problems?

....
....

Q. What are the pros and cons of the solutions?

....
....

Q. Which of the solutions do you believe would be best based on the pros and cons?

....
....

Talking

Talking with a person that you trust is an important way to manage your thoughts and feelings as it can help you to:

| EXPRESS HOW YOU ARE FEELING | CHALLENGE YOUR THOUGHTS | IDENTIFY ALTERNATIVE WAYS TO COPE WITH SITUATIONS |

This will help to protect your Self-Esteem Vault and banish your Self-Esteem Thief. However, it should not be used purely as a way of seeking attention.

Q. Which of the following people do you think you could talk to?

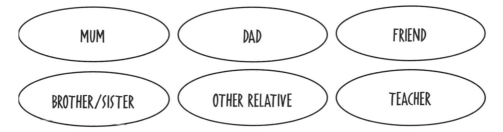

MUM   DAD   FRIEND

BROTHER/SISTER   OTHER RELATIVE   TEACHER

Q. Are there any other people who you would talk to and who aren't mentioned in the previous question? If so, write them down here.

....

....

Don't forget you can also talk to a professional, such as a doctor, psychologist or counsellor about your self-esteem issues either face to face or through a telephone helpline. Remember, talking can help you to banish your Self-Esteem Thief and build positive self-esteem.

Changing your 'self-talk'

Being aware of your self-talk (how you talk about yourself) will help you to protect your Self-Esteem Vault and banish your Self-Esteem Thief. Your self-talk needs to be realistic and positive, just as your thoughts do. Have a go at answering the questions in the following Self-Esteem Box to help you identify what your own 'self-talk' is like and how you can change this for the better.

SELF-ESTEEM BOX

What words do you currently use when talking about yourself to other people?

....
....
....
....

What effects does your self-talk have on you?

....
....
....
....

How could you improve your self-talk?

....
....
....
....

Living healthily

Eating a healthy balanced diet, getting regular exercise (but not too much) and getting adequate sleep can help you to:

- relax and de stress
- feel better physically
- feel rested.

These in turn can help you to concentrate better, think more clearly and feel more able to tackle situations. In addition, looking after yourself well can also make you feel more positive about yourself as it can provide you with a sense of achievement. Thus, living healthily can help you to protect your Self-Esteem Vault, banish your Self-Esteem Thief and improve your self-esteem. To help you with this, go online or to the library to find out the answers to the questions in the following Self-Esteem Box.

SELF–ESTEEM BOX

What does a healthy balanced diet involve?

....
....
....
....
....

What does a healthy amount of exercise involve?

....
....
....
....
....

What does a healthy amount of sleep involve?

....
....
....
....
....

You have now learnt how to manage your self-defeating behaviours and implement constructive behaviours as part of your overall behavioural management. Doing these helps you to protect your Self-Esteem Vault and banish your Self-Esteem Thief, as you have also learnt. Write down your managing behaviour goals in the next Self-Esteem Box.

SELF-ESTEEM BOX

My managing behaviours goal

Good luck with meeting these goals, protecting your Self-Esteem Vault and banishing your Self-Esteem Thief!

12

Self-Esteem Dos and Don'ts

Now it's time for you to think about everything you have learnt so far to help you to come up with your own personal list of Self-Esteem Dos and Don'ts. Write at least five of each in the following Self-Esteem Box. Remember that the Dos will banish your Self-Esteem Thief! Then write down the impacts that you think these Dos and Don'ts would have on you.

Some people find it helpful to carry this list around with them in their bag or to put a copy of it up on their wall at home so that they can look at it and remind themselves of what to do at times when they are finding their Self-Esteem Thief difficult to banish!

SELF-ESTEEM BOX

DOS	DON'TS

IMPACTS	IMPACTS

Here's an example of a Dos and Don'ts list from Darren, aged 12 years.

SELF—ESTEEM BOX

DOS	DONT'S
Accept myself for who I am. Accept that it is OK to make mistakes. Realise that perfection doesn't exist. Stop avoiding situations. Stop comparing myself to other people. Realise that we are all different and that is OK. Recognise my positive characteristics and my strengths. Be proud of me. Remember I am worthy. Put positive and realistic thoughts in my Self-Esteem Vault. Protect my Vault with constructive behaviours.	Avoid situations. Doubt myself all the time. Think in unrealistic ways about myself. Tell myself that I have to be perfect. Tell myself that people won't like me for who I really am. Tell myself that mistakes make me a failure. Compare myself negatively with others. Focus on my weaknesses. Tell myself I am useless and worthless. Fill my Vault with negative and unrealistic thoughts.

IMPACTS	IMPACTS
I will be happier in general. I will be able to do the things I want to do. I will reduce my anxiety and stress. I will believe in myself. I will be confident and assertive. I will be building my self-esteem. I will be protecting my Vault. I will eventually banish my Self-Esteem Thief! I will like me!	I will hate myself. I will want to change myself. I will be unhappy and miserable. I will worry my parents. I will regret the fact that I haven't done the things that I want to. I will be anxious and stressed. I will believe I can't do so many things. I will have low self-esteem. I will have left my Vault vulnerable to the Self-Esteem Thief!

13

Summing Up!

We have now gone through all the methods you may need to banish your Self-Esteem Thief and build positive self-esteem. It's now down to you to put them into practice. But don't forget you may not need them all. Just work on implementing those that are relevant to you and your self-esteem.

Remember...

Only YOU can change how you think and feel about yourself!

Only YOU can change how you act in response

to those thoughts and feelings!

YOU'RE the one in control of your self-esteem!

YOU have all the power to banish your Self-Esteem Thief!

Let's have a quick recap before we finish.

Write down five things that you have learnt about your self-esteem and how to build it in the following Self-Esteem Box.

SELF–ESTEEM BOX

What I have learnt

Let's also check what you have learnt by taking a Self-Esteem Quiz!

THE SELF-ESTEEM QUIZ!

1. **Where can you store your thoughts and feelings about yourself? Tick your answer.**

    a) The Self-Esteem Safe ☐   c) The Self-Esteem Hole ☐

    b) The Self-Esteem   ☐   d) The Self-Esteem Vault ☐
       Tunnel

2. **Unravel the word to find out who wants to steal your positive self-esteem.**

    HTE LFES-TEMESE HIFTE

3. **Name four types of self-defeating behaviours.**

    1. ....
    2. ....
    3. ....
    4. ....

4. **Which of the following can have a potential influence on your self-esteem? Tick your answers.**

    a) Life experiences   ☐   c) Societal messages   ☐

    b) Your interactions with ☐   d) Your personality   ☐
       others

5. **What do you need to do to your Self-Esteem Thief? Tick your answer.**

    a) Keep him around   ☐   b) Banish him   ☐

6. Name two aspects of your life that low self-esteem can impact on.

1.

2.

7. Name three types of thinking errors.

1.

2.

3.

8. Unravel this word to reveal something that people with low self-esteem can sometimes lack.

CENDIFNOCE

9. Self-esteem is how you . . . . and feel about yourself. What is the missing word? Tick your answer.

a) Ask   ☐   c) Think   ☐

b) Tell   ☐   d) Voice   ☐

10. Name three ways to help banish your Self-Esteem Thief.

1.

2.

3.

Turn to the Appendix to see how you've got on!

Well done! I'm sure you did brilliantly!

Now have a go at advising two other young people on their self-esteem issues, again to see just how much you have learnt about self-esteem while working through this book.

SELF-ESTEEM AUNT OR UNCLE!
LETTER 1

Imelda is 14 years old. She wants to be perfect at everything she does. She wants to get things right so that people will like her. She wants to please everyone, especially her parents. She also wants her boyfriend to think she looks perfect. But Imelda is falling apart under the pressure she is placing on herself. She cannot stop thinking about how she isn't doing well enough at everything. Imelda works even harder at things to try and get closer to her goal of perfection, but still doesn't succeed. Imelda now believes that she is worthless because she cannot achieve perfection and that her boyfriend will dump her, and her parents will stop loving her.

Write down below the advice that you would give to Imelda.

....
....
....
....
....
....
....
....
....
....
....
....
....
....
....
....
....
....
....
....
....
....

SELF-ESTEEM AUNT OR UNCLE!
LETTER 2

Ian is ten years old. He doesn't like who he is. He hates the fact that he wears glasses, has spots and is shorter than other boys his age. He feels that everyone else is better than him. Ian recently started a new school and feels different from the other boys there because he likes chess and going on walks, while they like computer games and playing football. Ian wishes that he could be different every day. He cannot understand why anyone at the new school would want to be friends with him so he hides away in the classroom at break times instead of going out to the playground to make friends.

Write down below the advice that you would give to Ian.

....
....
....
....
....
....
....
....
....
....
....
....
....
....
....
....
....
....
....

Now have a go at a more creative way of reinforcing what you have learnt with the following activity. If you wanted to spread the word about building positive self-esteem far and wide to children and young people, what would you do? Pick whether you would:

- design a website for children and/or young people to access

- design a poster campaign for schools and/or colleges

- design scenes for an advert aimed at children and/or young people

- give a talk in schools and/or colleges

- deliver a play in schools and/or colleges.

Then in the next box, jot down ideas on the kinds of things you would include. And if you want to have a go at completing your campaign advert, poster, website, etc. on some separate paper or on a computer, go ahead. Just think, your school or college may want to use it!

TEACHING CHILDREN AND YOUNG PEOPLE ABOUT SELF-ESTEEM!

Now let's check on how your self-esteem has changed during the course of reading this book by re-taking the My Self-Esteem Questionnaire. You will notice that there are now extra questions at the end! Have a go at answering the questions to see how well you've been banishing your Self-Esteem Thief.

MY SELF-ESTEEM QUESTIONNAIRE

1. **How often do you believe in yourself? Tick which answer applies to you.**

   a) Most of the time   ☐   d) Rarely   ☐

   b) A lot of the time   ☐   e) Never   ☐

   c) Occasionally   ☐

2. **How often do you feel confident in your abilities? Tick which answer applies to you.**

   a) Most of the time   ☐   d) Rarely   ☐

   b) A lot of the time   ☐   e) Never   ☐

   c) Occasionally   ☐

3. **How often do you worry about what other people think about you? Tick which answer applies to you.**

   a) Most of the time   ☐   d) Rarely   ☐

   b) A lot of the time   ☐   e) Never   ☐

   c) Occasionally   ☐

4. **How different is the 'real' you from how you would like to be? Tick which answer applies to you.**

   a) Completely different   ☐   c) A little different   ☐

   b) Quite a bit different   ☐   d) No different   ☐

5. **The table below contains a list of negative thoughts and beliefs that people with low self-esteem can have about themselves. Tick any that you agree with.**

THOUGHT OR BELIEF	I AGREE
I am not a worthy person	
Other people think I am unattractive	
I am a failure	
The first things that people notice about me are my flaws	
I am unattractive	
I am useless	
If I am not perfect, then I am a worthless person	
I am unlikeable and unlovable	
If I'm not perfect, no one will ever love me	
I am not good enough	
I must be perfect	
I wish I was someone different	
I would change lots of things about me if I could	
If I was a better person, I would be happier	
No one will ever like me unless I change things about myself	

THOUGHT OR BELIEF	I AGREE
I am not as worthy as other people	
I am not equal to other people	
Everyone else is better than me	
If I didn't hide the 'real' me, people wouldn't like me	
I need to look perfect for people to like me	
I need to be perfect for people to like me	
I don't have any good qualities	
I don't have many good qualities	
The only way to feel better is to change things about me	
If people knew the 'real' me, they would reject me	
I have too many weaknesses	
My weaknesses make me a failure	
I'm not a good enough person if I make mistakes	
If things go wrong, it means I'm not good enough	
If I'm not perfect, my life will be ruined	
I don't have much to be proud of about myself	
I dislike most things about myself	
My opinions don't matter	

THOUGHT OR BELIEF	I AGREE
My thoughts and feelings don't matter	
I don't matter	
I'm not competent enough	
Other people think I'm worthless	
Other people think I'm useless	
Other people think I'm a failure	
Other people think I'm unlikeable	
Things never go right for me	
Things will always go wrong for me	
Other people's needs, opinions and feelings are more important than mine	
If I'm not good at something, it means I'm stupid or useless or a failure	
People are only trying to make me feel better when they pay me compliments	

6. Do you lack confidence in yourself and your abilities in any of the situations listed below? Tick any that apply to you.

SITUATION	APPLIES TO ME
Parties	
Performing or speaking in front of others	
Voicing your opinion	
Taking exams	
School or college assignments	
Certain subjects at school or college	
Asking someone out on a date	
Going out on a date	
Making friends	
Hanging out with friends	
Dealing with conflict or disagreements	
Speaking to people	
Giving someone feedback on something	
Making a complaint	
Asking for help	

SITUATION	APPLIES TO ME
Leisure activities	
Sporting activities	
Speaking to family members	
Working towards future goals and ambitions	
Doing something new	
Learning something new	
Meeting new people	
Meeting other people's expectations	
Dealing with a problem	
Responding to people who treat you with disrespect	
Making decisions	
When needing to say 'no' to someone	
Standing up for your rights	
Other situations (please specify)	

7. Do your thoughts about yourself and your abilities cause you to feel any of the following? Highlight or colour in any that apply to you.

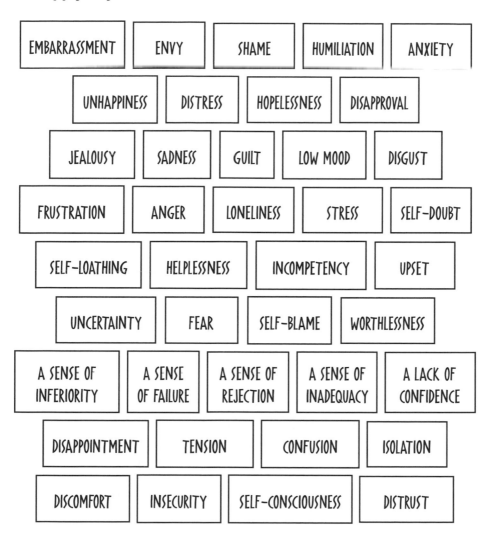

EMBARRASSMENT — ENVY — SHAME — HUMILIATION — ANXIETY

UNHAPPINESS — DISTRESS — HOPELESSNESS — DISAPPROVAL

JEALOUSY — SADNESS — GUILT — LOW MOOD — DISGUST

FRUSTRATION — ANGER — LONELINESS — STRESS — SELF-DOUBT

SELF-LOATHING — HELPLESSNESS — INCOMPETENCY — UPSET

UNCERTAINTY — FEAR — SELF-BLAME — WORTHLESSNESS

A SENSE OF INFERIORITY — A SENSE OF FAILURE — A SENSE OF REJECTION — A SENSE OF INADEQUACY — A LACK OF CONFIDENCE

DISAPPOINTMENT — TENSION — CONFUSION — ISOLATION

DISCOMFORT — INSECURITY — SELF-CONSCIOUSNESS — DISTRUST

8. Do you regularly worry about experiencing any of the following? Highlight or colour in any that apply to you.

HUMILIATION — FAILURE — REJECTION — BEING JUDGED NEGATIVELY BY OTHERS

9. **The table below contains a list of what we call 'self-defeating' behaviours. Tick any that you regularly do because of your thoughts and feelings about yourself.**

BEHAVIOUR	APPLIES TO ME
Avoid people	
Avoid certain types of situations	
Put off or avoid doing things	
Put off or avoid making decisions	
Avoid voicing your opinion	
Avoid expressing your feelings, wishes or needs	
Escape from situations that you are in	
Quit part way through doing things	
Hide aspects of yourself from others	
Try to please other people	
Try to be in 100 per cent control of a situation	
Work to excess	
Act aggressively towards others	
Act aggressively towards yourself	
Agree with others even though you don't really agree with them	

BEHAVIOUR	APPLIES TO ME
Agree to do things you don't want to do to please others instead of saying 'no'	
Say 'sorry' even though you have done nothing wrong	
Put yourself down when you speak	
Put your opinions down when you speak	
Avoid dealing with conflict	
Avoid dealing with problems	
Avoid dealing with situations where someone treats you or your rights with disrespect	
Allow others to get away with doing things you asked them not to do	
Use unconfident body language	
Use aggressive body language	
Seek reassurance from others about you and your abilities	
Seek sympathy from others	
Get other people to do things for you	
Do risky or dangerous things to prove yourself to others	

10. Your answers to the previous questions may show that you have negative thoughts and feelings about yourself and that you can act in self-defeating ways as a result. If so, have these had negative effects on any of the following aspects of your life? Highlight or colour in any that apply to you.

SOCIAL AND LEISURE ACTIVITIES	STUDIES AND WORK	FRIENDSHIPS	GOALS FOR THE FUTURE
PHYSICAL HEALTH	FAMILY RELATIONSHIPS	MENTAL HEALTH AND EMOTIONAL WELL-BEING	ROMANTIC RELATIONSHIPS

11. Do you believe that building positive self-esteem is in or out of your control? Tick which answer applies to you.

a) In my control ☐   b) Out of my control ☐

12. Have you seen any changes in your self-esteem since you completed the My Self-Esteem Questionnaire at the start of the book? Tick which answer applies to you.

a) Yes ☐   b) No ☐

13. If you have seen changes in your self-esteem, what are they?

....
....
....

14. What goals would you like to set yourself so that you can continue to improve your ability to banish your Self-Esteem Thief?

....
....
....

As you continue to put everything you have learnt from this workbook into practice, occasionally ask yourself the questions from the My Self-Esteem Questionnaire to monitor how far you have progressed and how well you're banishing your Self-Esteem Thief! Also, keep re-visiting the activities in the workbook to help you along the way.

But please be patient with yourself when putting all you've learnt into practice. You won't change everything overnight and remember, no one gets it right all the time. Perfection doesn't exist!

Also, remember that you have to keep working on filling your Self-Esteem Vault with realistic and positive thoughts and feelings and to protect your Self-Esteem Vault using constructive behaviours. This is especially important when you are facing difficult life circumstances or you are feeling stressed or worried in some way, as these are the times when we are more susceptible to relapsing into low self-esteem again because we are more likely to:

- place a few negative or unrealistic thoughts into our Vault

- act in self-defeating ways, thus blowing a bulb in our Vault's security camera or weakening a hinge in our Vault door.

But guess what? Even if you have a temporary slip up, even if you throw a few negative thoughts about yourself into your Vault and even if you delay starting a school assignment because of a belief that you won't be able to do it, thus blowing a bulb or weakening a hinge, it's not the end of the world!

Yes OK, the Self-Esteem Thief is a sneaky individual. He will be waiting around hoping for you to weaken your Vault's defence system in some way. He will be keeping his eyes peeled for a faulty lock or a loose chain in the hope that it's a sign of the whole defence system breaking down. This is because he wants you to let him back in again. He wants to steal all the positives from your Self-Esteem Vault once more. But this does not mean that he can actually do this.

You see, one blown camera bulb does not equal a broken defence system, as you still have all your other defences in place. And one blown camera bulb can be replaced with a new one, banishing your Self-Esteem Thief once more!

And don't forget, a few negative thoughts cannot take over your Self-Esteem Vault unless *you* allow the Thief in to steal the positive ones, leaving plenty of space for the negative ones to multiply! And you have the power to push a few negative thoughts back into that dark, musty, dusty, cobwebby corner of the Vault where they belong!

So even when times are difficult...

YOU are in control of your self-esteem!

YOU can banish your Self-Esteem Thief!

Just believe in YOU! Good luck!

This is to certify that

....

has successfully completed the
Banish Your Self-Esteem Thief
workbook and can expertly

BANISH THEIR
SELF-ESTEEM THIEF!

APPENDIX

THE SELF-ESTEEM QUIZ ANSWERS

1. (d) The Self-Esteem Vault.

2. The Self-Esteem Thief.

3. You may have included any of the behaviours discussed in Chapter 7, including avoidance behaviours and passive behaviours.

4. You should have ticked (a), (b), (c) and (d) as all of them can have a potential influence on your self-esteem.

5. (b) Banish him.

6. You may have listed any of the impacts discussed in Chapter 8, such as mental health and relationships.

7. You may have included any of the thinking errors discussed in Chapter 5, such as magnification and catastrophising.

8. Confidence.

9. (c) Think.

10. You may have included any of the 13 Steps towards building positive self-esteem discussed in Chapter 9, such as understanding what self-esteem means. You may also have included any of the managing thoughts strategies from Chapter 10, such as realistic thinking and any of the managing behaviours strategies from Chapter 11, such as graded exposure.

INFORMATION FOR PARENTS AND PROFESSIONALS

The purpose of this workbook

Banish Your Self-Esteem Thief provides a cognitive behavioural and mindfulness approach to building positive self-esteem for young people. It is designed for young people to work through on their own or with the support of a parent or a professional, such as a mental health practitioner, teacher, mentor, teaching assistant, social worker, doctor or youth worker.

This workbook provides self-help tools that can enable both males and females aged 10–18 years to build positive self-esteem whether their self-esteem is low overall or whether it is only low in specific situations. *Banish Your Self-Esteem Thief* can also help young people whose self-esteem is currently positive to keep it that way for the future.

However, it is important to note that although this workbook provides self-help tools that can be suitable for young people with varying levels of self-esteem issues, it should not be considered a substitute for treatment by a mental health professional where required. For example, it is recommended that young people seek immediate support from a mental health professional if their low self-esteem is particularly chronic; is accompanied by other mental health issues, such as depression, anxiety, eating disorders or suicidal ideations; is accompanied by negative coping strategies, such as substance misuse or self-harming; or has resulted from abuse, trauma or victimisation. *Banish Your Self-Esteem Thief* can be used as an accompaniment to treatment with a professional for maximum benefits in these types of cases.

This workbook can also provide useful information for those individuals wishing to learn more about self-esteem in order to help support a family member or friend.

Furthermore, although the self-help materials included in this workbook do not constitute a session-by-session therapeutic programme, they can be a useful resource for therapists working with young people. In this regard, it is important to note that the My Self-Esteem Questionnaire in Chapter 2 is a tool for young people to use to explore and gain a better understanding of their own self-esteem, but it is not designed to be used as a clinical diagnostic tool.

What is cognitive behavioural therapy?

Cognitive behavioural therapy (CBT) is an evidence-based, skills-based, structured form of psychotherapy, which emerged from Beck's Cognitive Therapy (Beck 1976) and Ellis' Rational-Emotive Therapy (Ellis 1962), as well as from the work of behaviourists such as Pavlov (Pavlov 1927) and Skinner (Skinner 1938) on classical and operant conditioning, respectively. CBT looks at the relationships between our thoughts (cognition), our feelings (emotions) and our actions (behaviours). It is based on the premise that how we interpret experiences and situations has a profound effect on our behaviours and emotions.

CBT focuses on:

- the problems that the client is experiencing in the present

- why the problems are occurring

- what strategies the client can use in order to address the problems.

The therapeutic process achieves this by empowering the client to identify:

- negative, unhealthy and unrealistic patterns of thoughts, perspectives and beliefs

- maladaptive and unhealthy patterns of behaviour

- the links between the problems the client is facing and their patterns of thoughts and behaviours

- how to challenge the existing patterns of thoughts and behaviours and implement alternative thoughts and behaviours that are constructive, healthy and realistic in order to address problems, manage emotions and improve well-being.

Thus the underlying ethos of CBT is that by addressing unhelpful patterns of thoughts and behaviours, people can change how they feel, how they view themselves, how they interact with others and how they approach life in general – thereby moving from an unhealthy cycle of reactions to a healthy one.

A wide range of empirical studies show CBT to be effective with many mental health disorders, including:

- body dysmorphic disorder (BDD) (Veale 1996, 2004)

- anxiety (Cartwright-Hatton *et al.* 2004; James, Soler and Weatherall 2005)

- obsessive compulsive disorder (OCD) (O'Kearney *et al.* 2006)

- depression (Klein, Jacobs and Reinecke 2007).

Low self-esteem can often exist alongside the disorders listed earlier, and some studies and systematic reviews are beginning to highlight the positive knock-on effects for low self-esteem when CBT is used with individuals with other such mental health disorders (Taylor and Montgomery 2009). However, although CBT is widely used in clinical practice with low self-esteem and although CBT-based self-help materials are available for low self-esteem sufferers to work through, empirical research studies into the effectiveness of CBT for self-esteem alone are still limited. Where these studies do occur, meta-analysis is showing promising results for CBT's effectiveness with self-esteem (Haney and Durlak 1998).

Effectiveness of CBT for children and young people

Although there has been less research conducted on the use of CBT with children and young people than there has been with adults, evidence for its effectiveness is continuing to grow and is reported in a number of reviews, such as Kazdin and Weisz (1998) and Rapee *et al.* (2000). Extensive research is still required on CBT and low self-esteem in children and young people, but where studies are available, meta-analysis is showing promising results (Haney and Durlak 1998). In addition, random clinical trials have shown CBT to be effective with children and young people for mental health disorders that often have low self-esteem existing alongside them, such as:

- OCD (Barrett, Healy-Farrell and March 2004)

- depression (Lewinsohn and Clarke 1999)

- generalised anxiety disorder (Kendall *et al.* 1997, 2004)

- specific phobias (Silverman *et al.* 1999)

- social phobia (Spence, Donovan and Brechman-Toussaint 2000)

- school refusal (King *et al.* 1998).

What is mindfulness?

Mindfulness originates from spiritual disciplines such as Buddhism and from practices such as meditation and yoga. The essence of mindfulness is that we can make a choice to:

- focus our attention on the present moment, thus engaging fully in the present with all our senses

- accept our thoughts and feelings as they are, thus observing them without criticism or judgement

- let those thoughts and feelings go, thus reducing any negative impact.

In the 1970s, mindfulness principles and practices were incorporated into a form of training known as mindfulness-based stress reduction (MBSR) developed by Jon Kabat-Zinn.

In the 1990s, principles of mindfulness also emerged within psychotherapy and became known as mindfulness-based cognitive therapy (MBCT) for use with people with a history of depression.

The key principles of mindfulness detailed here are also now incorporated into acceptance and commitment therapy (ACT), a mindfulness and values-based form of behavioural therapy. ACT sees our 'private experiences' (namely our thoughts, feelings and physical sensations) as not harmful in themselves. What is seen as harmful within ACT is how we choose to respond to those private experiences, such as seeing them as reality (what ACT terms 'cognitive fusion') and avoiding experiencing these thoughts, feelings and physical sensations (known as experiential avoidance). Thus, as well as teaching us principles of acceptance and being fully present in the moment, ACT also teaches us to make a distinction between our 'private experiences' and reality (a process known as 'cognitive defusion') and to commit to action that enriches and nourishes our lives based on our values (known as values-consistent behaviours).

The empirical support for ACT as an effective form of treatment for mental health issues, such as anxiety and depression, is growing (Forman *et al.* 2007), and initial studies looking at the effectiveness of mindfulness training for self-esteem issues are also showing positive impacts (Pepping, O'Donovan and Davis 2013).

Effectiveness of mindfulness-based therapies for children and young people

Research on the use of mindfulness-based therapies with children and young people is still in its infancy. However, evidence supporting its use is growing, especially in relation to ACT (Greco *et al.* 2005; Murrell and Scherbarth 2006). Studies are showing support for the use of ACT for children and young people with depression (Hayes, Boyd and Sewell 2011), generalised anxiety disorder (Greco 2002), anorexia nervosa (Heffner, Sperry and Eifert 2002) and pain (Greco *et al.* under review). And research is beginning to highlight how ACT can help to address the links between body image concerns and disordered eating in young people (Greco and Blomquist 2006) and how MBSR programmes can help to improve self-esteem in children and young people (Biegel *et al.* 2009).

REFERENCES

Barrett, P., Healy-Farrell, L. and March, J.S. (2004) 'Cognitive-behavioural family treatment of childhood obsessive compulsive disorder: a controlled trial.' *Journal of the American Academy of Child and Adolescent Psychiatry* *43*, 1, 46–62.

Beck, A.T. (1976) *Cognitive Therapy and Emotional Disorders.* New York: International Universities Press.

Biegel, G.M., Brown, K.W., Shapiro, S.L. and Schubert, C.M. (2009) 'Mindfulness-based stress reduction for the treatment of adolescent psychiatric outpatients: a randomized clinical trial.' *Journal of Consulting and Clinical Psychology* 77, 855–866.

Cartwright-Hatton, S., Roberts, C., Chitsabesan, P., Fothergill, C. and Harrington, R. (2004) 'Systematic review of the efficacy of cognitive behaviour therapies for childhood and adolescent anxiety disorders.' *British Journal of Clinical Psychology 43*, 421–436.

Ellis, A. (1962) *Reason and Emotion in Psychotherapy*. New York: Lyle-Stuart. Elle/MSNBC (2003).

Forman, E.M., Hoffman, K.L., McGrath, K.B., Herbert, J.D., Brandsma, L.L. and Lowe, M.R. (2007) 'A comparison of acceptance- and control-based strategies for coping with food cravings: an analog study.' *Behaviour Research and Therapy 45*, 2372–2386.

Greco, L.A. (2002) *Creating a context of acceptance in child clinical and paediatric settings.* Paper presented at the annual meeting of the Association for the Advancement of Behavior Therapy, Reno, NV, USA.

Greco, L.A., Blackledge, J.T., Coyne, L.W. and Ehrenreich, J. (2005) 'Integrating Acceptance and Mindfulness into Treatments for Child and Adolescent Anxiety Disorders: Acceptance and Commitment Therapy as an Example.' In S.M. Orsillo and L. Roemer (eds) *Acceptance and Mindfulness-based Approaches to Anxiety: Conceptualization and Treatment*. New York: Springer Science.

Greco, L.A. and Blomquist, K.K. (2006) 'Body image, eating behaviour, and quality of life among adolescent girls: role of anxiety and acceptance processes in a school sample.' In K.S. Berlin and A.R. Murrell (Co-chairs) *Extending acceptance and mindfulness research to parents, families and adolescents: process, empirical findings, clinical implications and future directions*. Paper presented at the Association for Behavior and Cognitive Therapies, Chicago, IL, USA.

Greco, L.A., Blomquist, K.K., Acra, S. and Moulton, D. (2008) 'Acceptance and commitment therapy for adolescents with functional abdominal pain: results of a pilot investigation.' Cited in Greco, L.A. and Hayes, S.C. (2008) *Acceptance and Mindfulness Treatments for Children and Adolescents: A Practitioners' Guide.* Oakland, CA: New Harbinger Publications.

Haney, P. and Durlak, J.A. (1998) 'Changing self-esteem in children and adolescents: a meta-analytic review.' *Journal of Clinical Child Psychology* 27, 423–433.

Hayes, L., Boyd, C.P. and Sewell, J. (2011) 'Acceptance and commitment therapy for the treatment of adolescent depression: a pilot study in a psychiatric outpatient setting. *Mindfulness* 2, 86–94.

Heffner, H., Sperry, J. and Eifert, G.H. (2002) 'Acceptance and commitment therapy in the treatment of an adolescent female with anorexia nervosa: a case example.' *Cognitive and Behavioural Practice* 9, 232–236.

James, A.A.C.J., Soler, A. and Weatherall, R.R.W. (2005) 'Cognitive behavioural therapy for anxiety disorders in children and adolescents.' *Cochrane Database of Systematic Reviews, 4.* Art, CD004690. DOI: 10.1002/14651858.CD004690.pub2. Published online January 2009. Available at http://onlinelibrary.wiley.com/doi/10.1002/14651858. CD004690.pub2/otherversions.

Kazdin, A.E. and Weisz, J.R. (1998) 'Identifying and developing empirically supported child and adolescent treatments.' *Journal of Consulting and Clinical Psychology 66,* 19–36.

Kendall, P.C., Flannery-Schroeder, E., Panichelli-Mindel, S.M., Sotham-Gerow, M., Henin, A. and Warman, M. (1997) 'Therapy with youths with anxiety disorders: a second randomized clinical trial.' *Journal of Consulting and Clinical Psychology 18,* 255–270.

Kendall, P.C., Safford, S., Flannery-Schroeder, E. and Webb, A. (2004) 'Child anxiety treatment: outcomes in adolescence and impact on substance abuse and depression at 7.4 year follow-up.' *Journal of Consulting and Clinical Psychology 72,* 276–287.

King, N.J., Molloy, G.N., Heyme, D., Murphy, G.C. and Ollendick, T. (1998) 'Emotive imagery treatment for childhood phobias: a credible and empirically validated intervention?' *Behavioural and Cognitive Psychotherapy 26,* 103–113.

Klein, J.B., Jacobs, R.H. and Reinecke, M.A. (2007) 'A meta-analysis of CBT in adolescents with depression.' *Journal of the American Academy of Child and Adolescent Psychiatry 46,* 1403–1413.

Lewinsohn, P.M. and Clarke, G.N. (1999) 'Psychosocial treatments for adolescent depression.' *Clinical Psychology Review 19,* 329–342.

Murrell, A.R. and Scherbarth, A.J. (2006) 'State of the research and literature address: ACT with children, adolescents and parents.' *International Journal of Behavioral Consultation and Therapy 2,* 531–543.

O'Kearney, R.T., Anstey, K., von Sanden, C. and Hunt, A. (2006) 'Behavioural and cognitive behavioural therapy for obsessive compulsive disorder in children and adolescents.' *Cochrane Database of Systematic Reviews*, 4, CD004856. DOI: 10.1002/14651858.CD004856.pub2. Published online January 2010. Available at http://onlinelibrary.wiley.com/doi/10.1002/14651858.CD004856.pub2/abstract

Pavlov, I.P. (1927) *Conditioned Reflexes: An Investigation of the Physiological Activity of the Cerebral Cortex.* Translated and edited by G.V. Anrep. London: Oxford University Press.

Pepping, C.A., O'Donovan, A. and Davis, P.J. (2013) 'The positive effects of mindfulness on self-esteem.' *The Journal of Positive Psychology 8*, 376–386.

Rapee, R.M., Wignall, A., Hudson, J.L. and Schniering, C.A. (2000) *Treating Anxious Children and Adolescents: An Evidence-Based Approach.* Oakland, CA: New Harbinger Publications.

Silverman, W.K., Kurtines, W.M., Ginsburg, G.S., Weems, C.F., Rabian, B. and Setafini, L.T. (1999) 'Contingency management, self-control and education support in the treatment of childhood phobic disorders: a randomized clinical trial.' *Journal of Consulting and Clinical Psychology 67*, 675–687.

Skinner, B.F. (1938) *The Behavior of Organisms.* New York: Appleton-Century-Crofts.

Spence, S., Donovan, C. and Brechman-Toussaint, M. (2000) 'The treatment of childhood social phobia: the effectiveness of a social skills training-based cognitive behavioural intervention with and without parental involvement.' *Journal of Child Psychology and Psychiatry 41*, 713–726.

Taylor, T.L. and Montgomery, P. (2009) 'Can cognitive behavioural therapy increase self-esteem among depressed adolescents? A systematic review.' *Children and Youth Services Review 29*, 823–839.

Veale, D. (2004) 'Advances in a cognitive behavioural model of body dysmorphic disorder.' *Body Image: An International Journal of Research 1*, 113–125.

Veale, D., Boocock, A., Gournay, K., Dryden, W. *et al.* (1996) 'Body dysmorphic disorder: a survey of fifty cases.' *The British Journal of Psychiatry 169*, 196–201.